WE ALL GET TO PLAY

WE ALL GET TO PLAY

Alastair Mitchell-Baker

with The Gate team

Growing a culture and practice of healing in the local church

ISBN: 978-1-9160388-2-0
eBook: 978-1-9160388-3-7

ACKNOWLEDGEMENTS

Thanks to Becky Jesty ('Tree of Life' on the front cover), Rebecca Machin ('The Wave'), Jenny Whitfield, Sammy Horne, Ralph Mann and Yinka Oyekan for kind permission to use their paintings. Thanks to Michael Davis-Bater for help with photographs of the paintings, his testimony, and encouragement.

My thanks to all in The Gate for their wisdom, love, faith, examples, and encouragement.

Special thanks to all whose teaching and messages have contributed to my thinking and to the resources section at the end of the book. This includes Yinka Oyekan, Gareth Owen, Danni Malone, Jeremy Sharpe, Julian Richards, and Jo Moody. Gareth, in particular, developed the Bible-study material on inner healing.

Thanks to Dr Randy Clark and Jo Moody especially for your teaching, amazing role-modelling, and encouragement.

My particular thanks to Dr Roger Greene, Rev Lynn Green and Professor Richard Vincent for their detailed feedback, advice and encouragement, and to Jane for editing, encouragement, and long suffering!

The title *We All Get to Play* is attributed to John Wimber, who led the Vineyard movement and was committed to equipping and mobilising 'ordinary believers'.

FOREWORD

Through Alastair Mitchell-Baker's book *We All Get to Play: Growing Healing in the Local Church*, every reader will walk away understanding that as followers of Christ we not only have a biblical mandate to heal the sick and free those in bondage but that healing ministry as a body of believers is the greatest adventure we will ever have the pleasure of experiencing. He invites, challenges, and inspires each and every man, woman and child to do the greater things that Jesus said we would do as a matter of Christian lifestyle, and to advance the Kingdom of Heaven through our churches both small and large. A must read for church leadership!

Reverend Joanne Moody
Author of *Minute by Minute*, Founder of Agape Freedom Fighters

This is an accessible and vital piece of work that is thoroughly researched, clearly presented and comprehensively referenced. The author's humility and vision will inspire many to discover a realistic and practical ministry of healing that is the potential of not just a few, but of all who follow Jesus. Adopting the book's recommendations, and drawing on the experience and learning resources included, will be transformative for individual Christians as well as the fellowship and witness of the church.

Professor Richard Vincent BSc, MD, FRCP, AKC, EFESC
Emeritus Professor of Cardiology and Previous Founding Dean of Brighton Medical School, and Chief Executive of PRIME

What I love about this book is its challenge that we can all bring a measure of healing into people's lives, no matter what the degree, demonstrating God's goodness. I have watched Alastair pursue this grace of healing without shrinking back despite personal challenges, and community challenges, when it would have been easy to give up, holding on to truth above personal conflict – and because of that we are richer as a church family. This book is gold refined in the fire of proving that God is a God of miracles.

Yinka Oyekan
Senior Minister, The Gate, and International Team Leader, Barnabas fellowship of Churches

CONTENTS

Eagle, by Ralph Mann.
This graphic drawing depicts something of my journey over the last few years.
It was commissioned by a friend and coach, Richard Thorby.

INTRODUCTION

"But nothing worth having comes without some kind of fight,
Got to kick at the darkness 'til it bleeds daylight"
From Lovers in a Dangerous Time, *written by Bruce Cockburn[1]*

This book is designed as a resource for church leaders and members who want to see more healing and transformation in their local churches and communities. It is born of my personal journey of the last five or so years and the experiences and teaching of The Gate Church in 2017. I recognise that the subject of healing can be contentious and challenging. Our experiences can often leave us with many questions, so I have tried not to duck the difficult issues. My prayer is this book will challenge, inspire and equip you and your church family to pursue healing and wholeness.

THE CHILDREN'S BREAD IS FOR EVERYONE

In Matthew 15:22-28 Jesus describes healing and deliverance as the 'children's bread'. In other words, it is an everyday essential that no good father would withhold from his children. How much more so does our Father God want to bless us today with these gifts? My fundamental desire is to close the gap between what we read in the New Testament description of Jesus and the early church's

---

1 *Lovers in a Dangerous Time* written by Bruce Cockburn. Copyright © 1984 Golden Mountain Music Corp. Controlled and administered by Songs of Universal, Inc. All rights reserved.

ministry and kingdom lifestyle, and our experiences as individual believers and, especially, as the family of God in our churches.

Our churches are of all types, styles and sizes. We look wonderfully and beautifully different, and so the full restoration of healing ministry will look and feel different too. We will not all look the same, but I believe Jesus wants us all to be His feet and hands, His eyes, ears, and lips to bring His restoring love and power to other people in our communities, towns and cities.

Healing might look like my friend[2] who had a torn diaphragm, which a consultant surgeon said was repairable only by invasive surgery. After prayer she was encouraged to take daily communion and, two weeks later, the tear was gone! Or it might look like Sandy, who I prayed with after a service in Chorleywood. After some brief prayer for inner healing and release of trauma, all the pain in her back from an accident went! Or it's a stranger in a supermarket bent over in pain. With their permission, we pray and command all pain to go. It does – the look of joyous surprise is to treasure!

I also believe God wants us to have a fresh confidence and understanding of how we can partner with medical and allied professionals to bring healing and care to people. God heals in so many ways, as we shall see later. Medicine, and related disciplines, is a critical God-given method for healing. We need to work respectfully with professionals, so for instance if someone believes they are healed after prayer, we always advise them to keep taking any prescribed medications until they have seen their own doctor.

---

2 The names and identifying details of people have been changed in the stories and testimonies used in the book, except where people have given permission to be identified.

Introduction

Doctors might understand and explain in various ways what has happened if people are healed: 'spontaneous remission,' 'it must have been psychosomatic' or sometimes even, 'that sounds like a miracle'! Generally, however, they are always pleased for their patients to get better!

In the first week of the first Turning[3] mission (before it was so called) I was telling a friend of all that was happening. I had a picture of Jesus weeping over the UK, preparing the ground as it were for the harvest to come. We've begun to see it, but we need to deliberately prepare ourselves for more to come. This is not a call for striving. We don't need to work harder or to do more to 'persuade' God to pour out His grace. We can prepare for 'the more' by growing our capacity and deliberately positioning ourselves ready for His move. This book seeks to help churches do that in respect of healing.

I think churches can move more powerfully into the healing ministry collectively, than just by a few committed individuals. Although, I salute all my friends across the globe who have persevered, pushed through rejection and scorn, and seen their churches released into freedom! As church bodies, we can pray together, and critically move together under a spiritual covering of aligned and supportive leadership.

Almost every church denomination has been birthed in, and generally experienced, the powerful move of the supernatural including healing and deliverance.[4] My reading, and experience,

---

3 'The Turning' is an evangelistic move of God which started in 2016 in the Gate church in Reading and has now seen many city-wide, regional and national missions. http://theturning.eu/

4 See Dr Randy Clarke, 'Healing Streams', for a sympathetic exploration of what each church tradition has brought.

over the last few years has given me a fresh appreciation and gratitude for the Roman Catholic and Pentecostal traditions which were probably farthest from my own experience growing up as an Anglican and, latterly, worshipping as a Baptist. So often, these historical moves of God have been 'closed down' as things became formalised and 'religious' practice dominated. However, many people believe we live in unprecedented times of fresh renewal across the world.

AUTHENTICITY: LEARNING TO EMBRACE MYSTERY

In our twenty-first-century world of 'virtual' connection and 'fake news', people want to see and experience things for themselves. People want to know and experience God for themselves. There is a need for authentic true expression of kingdom life in and through us as we seek to bring healing. In this, as we reflect Jesus, we must seek in His grace to be always honest and truthful. To never manipulate. To persevere and be faithful. And to always, always move in love.

Not everyone is healed. I don't know why. But I have chosen to trust God. He is good, utterly good. So, I trust Him, and choose to keep persevering. I have developed the concept of a 'mystery box', which I imagine to be by my side and into which I put things I don't understand, such as when people die, or are not healed (see chapter 6). My God is big enough for any and all mysteries. As I press in for more, I may understand more of why people might not be healed and what I could do differently, but I will never know enough to satisfy my rational mind, especially as my first career was as a scientist. But I know who my Father is, and I trust Him.

My 'mystery box' is not just for things that concern, or cause, pain. They can include amazing things like the 'sky angel'. During my sabbatical in 2014, I went on a five-day silent retreat at a Jesuit retreat centre. I was on a long walk in the hills, talking with the Lord about Revelation 21 and the glory of the nations being taken into heaven. I started thinking about the work I do in my company (a Christian consulting company based on Isaiah 61[5]) and I realised I needed the full 'right' and 'left' sides of my brain – my rational/logical and artistic/creative sides. I had tended to ignore the latter.

I did some 'ministry', using 'restoring the foundations' (a form of inner healing) on myself. I identified, renounced, and confessed my wrong thinking and ungodly beliefs, forgave others and myself, asked for healing of any wounds or hurts in my spirit/soul, delivered myself of any 'wrong spirits' and asked for the Holy Spirit's help.

I will never forget rounding the corner on the brow of the hill. There in the sky over the valley was a 'sky angel' – a staggeringly beautiful cloud in the shape of a classic angel with a head made up of half a rainbow. I stood in wide-eyed amazement. It was, I am sure, a pointer, a sign from the Lord in response to our conversation. I couldn't photograph it as I had no phone with me but I did try to paint it and write a poem! The memory and mystery lives with me still.

Pursuing Christ's call to be a healing church will be full of joy and sorrow, highs and lows, adventure and excitement, and

---

5   My colleague Dr Roger Greene has written a great book about the Christian call to the marketplace including our company, called *How On Earth Did That Happen?* (Great Big Life Publishing, 2016).

ultimately of mystery, as we follow the Lord. I invite you to join me in on the journey.'

STRUCTURE OF THIS BOOK

The book is designed as a resource for churches and leaders seeking to start and/or grow the healing ministry. The chapters seek to cover the core ground related to where any individual church is in its journey. Recognising we all have different learning styles, I have included a mix of biblical context and teaching, practical 'how to' guidance, real life stories, small group Bible-study material, and links to online video and audio messages.

- Chapter 1 – **The commission to heal.** Exploring how we are called as individual believers and churches to bring the Kingdom of God, including healing, on earth.
- Chapter 2 – **Where are we now?** Exploring and assessing where our churches are and how we can develop our church's practice and culture in healing.
- Chapter 3 – **Does God heal today?** The biblical basis for healing today including exploring cessationism. Much of this chapter can be skipped if it does not feel relevant!
- Chapter 4 – **Restoring biblical belief and practice.** Outlining what the Bible says about why God heals and how we can lead our churches into this.
- Chapter 5 – **Overcoming fear: dealing with disappointment.** How we keep soft hearts before God

in the face of disappointment and struggles.

- Chapter 6 – **A simple model for praying for the sick: HEAL.** How we can pray for the sick.
- Chapter 7 – **Getting going with healing: words of knowledge.** Explaining what they are and how you receive and move in them.
- Chapter 8 – **Growing together: spiritual and inner healing.** Introducing inner/emotional healing and deliverance within an overall balanced healing ministry.
- Chapter 9 – **The Invitation: keys to growing in healing.** Key principles which can help us grow in healing.
- **Appendix/Resources** – Links to online messages, recommended resources, and notes for group study and activation sessions.

1

THE COMMISSION TO HEAL

"Earth's crammed with heaven,
And every common bush afire with God;
But only he who sees, takes off his shoes,
The rest sit round it and pluck blackberries."

From Aurora Leigh
by Elizabeth Barrett Browning (1806-1861)

RESPONDING TO THE CALL: A NIGHT IN THE JUNGLE

I have found myself drawn to the healing ministry over the last few years. I don't know why. I was always scared of it. Unlike most other ministries, you could see the results – very visibly, very tangibly. People were either healed or not. I would pray but never ever ask if anything had happened. I was an Elder for many years (and still am), and so there was an expectation that I /we would pray for people. We would indeed pray at church, and see people healed sometimes. I remember, many years ago, praying for my nephew in my local hospital where I used to work, after he fell out of a tree, and despite the medical prognosis of kidney damage, he had no ongoing problems.

Then in 2014 I had the privilege of a two-month sabbatical

from my company. After a week's prayer ministry,[6] three weeks in the US which included going to a Bethel Leaders Advance as a family, a five-day silent retreat at a Jesuit Centre[7] and some precious family time, I decided to follow the advice I had heard from several people: 'If you really want to get into healing, go to Brazil with Dr Randy Clark.'[8] So I did, in December 2014. It was transformative. I had a tough couple of days where I could not seem to even pray for a headache to leave someone and yet other team members were seeing all sorts of healings and miracles. Then there was an evening I will never forget, in the 'church in the jungle' on the edge of Londrina, a city to the south of Brazil.

The pattern was that of most nights with worship followed by Dr Randy talking and showing videos of prior healings. During his talk several of us were praying and interceding in a back room. We rejoined the meeting at the end of his talk and heard that many people were healed just from watching the videos and hearing of what God had done before! Another reason to share testimony! Dr Randy then asked each team member to bring a word of knowledge each and we were then to pray for people. My word (to my horror, to be honest) was for a 'brain tumour'. A man came up in a wheelchair, incapacitated by a brain tumour. I prayed – there was no discernible change. At this stage I had not really seen as much as a headache healed all week in the people I'd prayed for, so although God was

---

6 With the amazing Restoring The Foundations ministry. https://www.restoringthefoundations.uk/

7 St Beuno's. Highly recommended. https://www.pathwaystogod.org/org/st-beunos

8 See https://globalawakening.com/ministry-trips

evidently at work all around me, I wondered whether this was really something I was indeed called to.

The next nine people I prayed for were all healed. Dramatically, obviously, and much to my surprise.

The first people were a mother and daughter. Both had spondylitis with obvious curvature of the spine and severe short-sightedness. I prayed for the mother first. Before I knew what was happening she fell to the floor under the Spirit and writhed around. She got up and her back was straight! And her eyesight was normal! I was gobsmacked! The same then happened to her daughter. This continued through the next hour or so. By the end of the evening when the church lady overseer/bishop came up for prayer with a frozen shoulder I had no doubts, and she was healed with full movement of her arms after two prayers.

My expectations and faith for healing were forever changed. I came back to the UK determined to see in my local church and own country the same as I had seen in Brazil.

Do I yet see it? Not fully but I *am* now surprised if people aren't healed. I am part of a church where nearly everybody knows how to pray for healing and how to lead people to the Lord!

HIS STORY

Jesus began His earthly ministry when He reached the traditional Jewish age of maturity at thirty in His hometown synagogue in Nazareth by reading the six-hundred-year-old prophecy of Isaiah.

*The Spirit of the Sovereign L*ORD *is on me, because the L*ORD *has anointed me to proclaim good news to the poor. He has sent me to bind up the broken-hearted, to proclaim freedom for the captives and release from darkness for the prisoners, to proclaim the year of the L*ORD*'s favour and the day of vengeance of our God, to comfort all who mourn, and provide for those who grieve in Zion – to bestow on them a crown of beauty instead of ashes, the oil of joy instead of mourning, and a garment of praise instead of a spirit of despair. They will be called oaks of righteousness, a planting of the L*ORD *for the display of his splendour. They will rebuild the ancient ruins and restore the places long devastated; they will renew the ruined cities that have been devastated for generations. (Isaiah 61:1-4)*

This was written to Israel at a time of crisis and exile – and, as with so many of Isaiah's writings, it operates on at least two levels. For the original hearers, it would have been heard as a promise of restoration from exile, and liberty from the oppression of enemies. It came to be understood in the years following Isaiah as also looking forward to the coming of God's anointed Son, the Messiah. It also echoed the words (now in Isaiah 53:4-5) of the suffering servant.

Surely, he took up our pain and bore our suffering, yet we considered him punished by God, stricken by him, and afflicted. But he was pierced for our transgressions, he was crushed for our iniquities; the punishment that brought us peace was on him, and by his wounds we are healed.

WE ALL GET TO PLAY

As Luke 4:18ff recounts, Jesus reading the scriptures was nothing unusual. What changed everything was His closing remark: 'Today this scripture is fulfilled in your hearing.' This was a startling claim to be the Messiah, the long-promised one, who would restore the people of Israel. So began the most action-packed, world-changing three years of human existence.

THE BIG STORY

The film *Monuments Men* tells the story of the last few months of the Second World War. It was clear which way things were going with the Allies fast approaching Germany. Word reached art curators that there were Nazi orders to destroy many lovely paintings and precious sculptures, which had been captured and hidden in mines by the Nazis. The Monument Men, led by George Clooney's character, had to find and secure these before the Germans found and destroyed them. The end result was clear: the war was going to be won, but there were still missions to be pursued and battles to fight that were critical for art and for people held in captivity and fear.

We have that same dual situation as Christians today. Jesus has won the war. Isaiah 53 tells of His finished work as the suffering servant who died for our sins – our salvation and for our diseases – our healing. The war is won, but there are battles to be fought – and we, His people, as believers and as the church, have been given a mandate to fight.

In the Old Testament we see the 'big story' unfold. From creation and the fall (Adam and Eve), through God blessing people who rebel, and bring destruction on themselves, only for remnant to be saved (Noah). Then God calls one man, Abraham, gives him a promise and, in response to Abraham's faith, blesses him and his family – Isaac and Jacob. God is always blessing and saving His people, even through Joseph and captivity in Egypt. Then four hundred years later the people of Israel end up in slavery, and yet God sends a prophet, Moses, who leads them to freedom – the exodus. During this desert wandering, God reveals Himself as Jehovah-Rapha, God the Healer.

> *He said, 'If you listen carefully to the LORD your God and do what is right in his eyes, if you pay attention to his commands and keep all his decrees, I will not bring on you any of the diseases I brought on the Egyptians, for I am the LORD, who heals you.' (Exodus 15:26)*

Sadly, the rebellion continues. The Israelites live as rebels again in the desert before finally entering the Promised Land across the Jordan under the leadership of Joshua. There they gradually drive out the indigenous people but compromise creeps in; their fortunes wax and wane as they choose to follow God or not. As they rebel again, God sends judges and then kings to rescue them. Saul, and then David, the worshipper, follow this pattern of obedience and rebellion. Israel's rebellion eventually leads to exile at the time of Isaiah. He prophesies of the Saviour, the Messiah to come as the Israelites' true King in Isaiah 9:6. Then Israel returns home to the Promised Land and there are four hundred years of biblical 'quiet'.

And then the Messiah, Jesus, is born and raised – thirty years of 'ordinary life', and then a time of testing in solitude before He announces His manifesto in Luke 4:14-21, as below. He lived and was crucified as Isaiah 53 had prophesied but rose again and inaugurates and empowers the church by sending the Holy Spirit.

> *Jesus returned to Galilee in the power of the Spirit, and news about him spread through the whole countryside. He was teaching in their synagogues, and everyone praised him. He went to Nazareth, where he had been brought up, and on the Sabbath day he went into the synagogue, as was his custom. He stood up to read, and the scroll of the prophet Isaiah was handed to him. Unrolling it, he found the place where it is written: 'The Spirit of the Lord is on me, because he has anointed me to proclaim good news to the poor. He has sent me to proclaim freedom for the prisoners and recovery of sight for the blind, to set the oppressed free, to proclaim the year of the Lord's favour.' Then he rolled up the scroll, gave it back to the attendant and sat down. The eyes of everyone in the synagogue were fastened on him. He began by saying to them, 'Today this scripture is fulfilled in your hearing.'*

We are then given a glimpse and a promise of His return, the second coming and of a restored heaven and earth in Revelation, culminating in the city of God. This is the 'in between' times we live in. This is the Big Story. His story of redemption, reconciliation, and restoration. Jesus came and called a people back to Himself. He calls us still to come to Him, His love for you and me is passionate and real.

We live in the 'Today' times of the Nazarene declaration in Luke 4. *'Today* this scripture is fulfilled in your hearing.' He inaugurated the coming of His Kingdom. He declared that the Year of Jubilee had come – permanently. He won the war, defeating sin and death on the cross, but He has called us to fight the battles, in His power, to complete the work of restoration, healing and freedom; life by life, precious person by precious person, people group by people group, and nation by nation.

This work, for me, stretches from the individual through the organisational to the societal and national transformation. Individual healing and change is needed *and* social action and justice. We create an un-biblical split if we focus on only one. Isaiah 61 speaks of individual freedom and change, as well as city transformation. As churches we have a role to teach and equip believers to bring the Kingdom in their everyday lives wherever they go, and at all levels from individual to culture.

Jesus has done it, so we work from His victory, but it's yet to be fully worked out – there's work for us to do. Like the Second World War and the Monuments Men.

OUR STORY

Jesus preached and demonstrated His kingdom had come with miracles, healing and deliverance. He also commissioned His twelve disciples to follow and continue His mission – and to do likewise. This call and commission was passed on to the seventy-two, and to all disciples.

The Commission to Heal

When Jesus had called the Twelve together, he gave them power
and authority to drive out all demons and to cure diseases, and
he sent them out to proclaim the kingdom of God and to heal
those who were ill. (Luke 9:1-2)

After this the Lord appointed seventy-two others and sent them
two by two ahead of him to every town and place where he was
about to go. He told them, 'The harvest is plentiful, but the workers
are few. Ask the Lord of the harvest, therefore, to send out workers
into his harvest field. Go! I am sending you out like lambs among
wolves. Do not take a purse or bag or sandals; and do not greet
anyone on the road ... Heal those who are ill and tell them, "The
kingdom of God has come near to you."' (Luke 10:1-4, 9)

It became the call and commission of the New Testament
church and now it's our call and our commission. Over the
last two thousand years the church, and its various branches,
have understood and interpreted this call in different ways. But
there is nothing I find in the whole of the Bible which revokes
the call and commission.[9]

The question is, will we as believers in our churches live it
out fully? Will we let the words and actions of Jesus set our
expectations? Or will we let our experiences thus far determine
our expectation?

In Isaiah 61 we see the Messiah as the anointed one who
comes to bring release. We see God's people restored (both
Israel, and now us as the people of God), then we are all called

---

9 See chapter 4 for a discussion of contrary views.

to be those who restore and build up others. We are given a new identity, and name, to reflect our new role.

Peter says in 1 Peter 2:4-5 we are priests and ministers of the gospel.

> *As you come to him, the living Stone – rejected by humans but chosen by God and precious to him – you also, like living stones, are being built into a spiritual house to be a holy priesthood, offering spiritual sacrifices acceptable to God through Jesus Christ.*

Jesus also commissions us to share His mission, and co-work and partner with Him. Mark 16:15-20 records it as follows:

> *He said to them, 'Go into all the world and preach the gospel to all creation. Whoever believes and is baptised will be saved, but whoever does not believe will be condemned. And these signs will accompany those who believe: in my name they will drive out demons; they will speak in new tongues; they will pick up snakes with their hands; and when they drink deadly poison, it will not hurt them at all; they will place their hands on people who are ill, and they will get well.' After the Lord Jesus had spoken to them, he was taken up into heaven and he sat at the right hand of God. Then the disciples went out and preached everywhere, and the Lord worked with them and confirmed his word by the signs that accompanied it.*

As Isaiah 61:10 says, this results in praise and worship!

Stepping out of the old, by Jenny Whitfield. Stepping out of our old comfortable shoes, onto new ground, into new things, onto Holy ground

WHOLE STORY

Isaiah's prophecy shows us the Father's heart. It restores and arouses hope. We are to be those who bring hope to others in difficult and tough times – who don't know how they are going to get through. We, knowing that our Father loves us and them, are to bring good news.

If the need is physical healing, restoration of sight or hearing: Jesus did it, the twelve did it, the seventy-two did it. We can do it. We must, as we are commanded to.

Suppose I am working at the local supermarket collecting trolleys in the car park. My boss has told me to collect all the trolleys and even move his car if needed – and has given me the keys. If I see the need to move his car but keep asking him for the keys – which I have already got – how will he feel?

Jesus has already given us the order (commission), and the keys (power and authority). Time to do it, and not keep questioning or, worse still, ignoring Him!

For many people the need is for inner, or emotional, healing, 'binding up the broken-hearted'. Lots of things happen in our lives, especially as we grow up, even in families who love and care for us. We can get hurt at a deep level even by family and friends and even (if not especially) by the church. Bad stuff happens to good/God's people. And then there's evil – we live in a fallen hostile world.

We need to live as those who do not take offence, and forgive quickly and always. If we don't, we can be open to spiritual attack. Many are unwittingly bound up. Many of us need help in inner, emotional, and relational healing.

SUMMARY

Jesus calls us all to freedom – freedom to be who we are called to be and live in relational harmony with others; to live in joy, and not sorrow. This extends beyond just our own individual and family lives but is a call for community and societal transformation – ruins and cities need healing and transformation too.

How are you and your church family going to respond to Jesus' call and commission to be agents of freedom and healing?

2

WHERE ARE WE NOW?

"If you want to go fast, go alone. If you want to go far, go with others."

African Proverb

PREPARING OUR CHURCHES FOR A FRESH WAVE OF GOD

My local church is The Gate, Reading. God moved in amazing ways in 2016 with an evangelistic outpouring that led to the birth of The Turning. In early 2017, we embarked on a six-month programme of pressing into teaching and activation in healing for the whole church. There is much we could have done better but we have seen a fundamental shift in the attitudes, experience and practice of healing in our church community.

I believe that every one of the fifty thousand or so churches in the UK (and every church in every nation) can, and are called to, become fully activated as local expressions of the body of Christ in healing. This is essential to obey Christ, and to fully and faithfully represent the love and power of God to a desperate and needy generation. Only by walking with Him, and ministering like Him, can we fulfil the Great Commission and bring the Kingdom of God to earth.

Many have prophesied that there is another wave of God's

grace coming to the UK, and indeed to Europe and the rest of the world. And this next wave includes healing, restoration, and freedom like never before! This book is offered as a resource to help churches position themselves to ride the wave of the Spirit!

THE LESSONS OF THE TURNING

The story of The Turning has been told elsewhere.[10] I recall praying before the mission that God would change me so that I had the same hunger and expectation in evangelism as I had grown to have in healing. I had come to expect everyone to be healed and am surprised if they are not. (Of course, not everyone is healed immediately, but more of that later.) Little did I realise just *how* the Lord would answer my prayers.

We planned as a church, initially, a week-long mission with American evangelist Tommy Zito and his team. Four weeks later the church was alight with an evangelistic grace we had not even dreamed about. Young and old, experienced, and brand-new Christians were leading people to Christ. We had so many lessons to learn about follow-up and discipleship but undoubtedly something significant had shifted spiritually. This evangelistic grace has continued across many cities and nations as we have trained, equipped, and activated 'ordinary' church members in street evangelism. It has been amazing to see the unity that has come as churches work together in mission.

The Gate is not a large church – we joke that we are the church 'God found down the back of the sofa'. There is nothing

---

10 See The Turning Learning Review 2016 http://theturning.eu/index.php/learning-review/ and Annual Review 2017 http://theturning.eu/index.php/2007-2/

exceptional about us that God would choose to pour His grace into and through us. We were in the right place at the right time. And we said 'yes'. We have seen the prayers of many answered. So often on the streets when someone prays and asks Christ into their life, when I ask them if someone has been praying for them, they tell me about a parent or, most often, a grandmother, who is praying for them. They know what they have done. They know they have come home.

There are four big things I have learnt from The Turning that I think are applicable to activating churches for the healing ministry:

- **Overcoming fear**: to move out in evangelism and/or healing, we need to move beyond our fear of others and of 'failing'.
- **Know-how**: we need to be equipped with simple practical tools to help us.
- **Power of unity**: there is a blessing in working together within, and across, churches.
- **Presence of God**: ultimately, it is only the presence of God and empowering through the Holy Spirit that can lead anyone to saving faith and into healing, deliverance, and freedom.

This book seeks to apply this learning to healing in, and through, churches.

ASSESSING WHERE YOU ARE AS A CHURCH

To lead our churches into greater understanding and experience

The Wave, Rebecca Machin

of healing, it is helpful if we can assess where we start from. In particular, to explore and reflect on our own understanding, beliefs, and practice. It may be helpful to initially do this outside our usual setting. The Bible and church history are full of people encountering God in life-changing ways when they are on a 'journey', 'mission' or just outside of their usual environment. You may, like me, have been essentially brought up in a 'soft cessationist' environment, where it is accepted God can heal sovereignly but healing is expected to be rare. The focus may be on explaining the 'pain of suffering' and loving people through pain and sickness. All vital but the danger is our focus and experience subtly sets our expectations. This is often reinforced by a pastorally based theology, to explain the gap between our experience and the New Testament. When we journey outside our usual everyday environment to other church traditions or countries we can often see and experience God working in surprisingly new and different ways. We can also 'see' ourselves more clearly.

We also need to share and discuss these questions with our fellow senior leaders, with whom we share responsibility and oversight for the spiritual health of our congregation(s). We may also reflect on where members of the congregation are too. The following questions are intended as 'prompts'.

- What do you believe about healing? Do you believe and expect God to heal today? Do you expect supernatural healing to be rare or common?
- How do you understand the Kingdom of God? What

do you understand to be 'the gospel'? Is it just 'good news' about our salvation or do you see healing and deliverance as also part of the gospel and the coming of the Kingdom of God?

- Do you expect God to use ordinary believers to heal people?
- How do you and your church usually pray for healing?
- What experiences, if any, have you had of supernatural healing?
- What supernatural healing(s) have you seen in the church body? Have these been shared and talked about?
- How often do you or others teach/preach about healing and related topics?
- Have there been cases where people who you or others have prayed for, and believed God would heal, were not healed, and even died? How did that make you feel? How did you deal with it? How has it affected your view of healing?
- What explicit opportunities do you have for healing prayer? E.g. special services, prayer teams, healing rooms?
- What's your approach to inner healing? Any stories to share?
- What's your understanding and experience of deliverance? Any stories? Are you or your church members concerned or fearful about deliverance?

Reflecting on these questions, you may want to identify where you think your church is in the following model. Theis is a simple 'growth model' which can help assess where your church is in respect of healing. It should not be seen as a judgement of where any church is but a guide to help identify what teaching, equipping, and encouragement might help it grow further.

0 Not for us	1 Dormant	2 Getting going	3 Growing together	4 Thriving body
God can heal but He chooses to do so rarely. We pray at home for sick members. Healing is not really for today and maybe God sends sickness to grow our characters.	We have and sometimes still do pray for the sick directly. But we have been disappointed and are afraid to be discouraged again. But we know God can heal.	Some people, especially our leaders in church, regularly do pray for people and we hear of people being healed. It's encouraging but you need to be special to pray for people.	Everybody is encouraged to pray for healing but only some do. We have a special ministry team and maybe even Healing Rooms. We talk about healing and hear people's stories quite often.	Virtually every member is confident in praying for sick people in the market place as part of their everyday lives as well as in church. People of all faiths and none seek out the church and ask for healing. There are regular stories and testimonies of healing in small groups, church meetings and online.

For a church body to grow in the practice of healing, I believe, it needs committed leadership who will ensure there is:

- **Good teaching.** People need to understand what the Bible says about healing from the life of Jesus and His disciples, and His commission and call to us as His body today to heal. For some this will involve dismantling some deeply entrenched and invidious misunderstandings and untruths picked up from church teaching over many years. For others, especially younger people and newer Christians, this may just need to be teaching and releasing them into truth.

- **Demonstration of healing and miracles.** As Paul said, our teaching must not just be words but we must walk in the reality of healing. It has taken time but I now quite often get 'words of knowledge' (see chapter 7 for more) as I am about to preach. I now share these and as people respond we get others around them to pray – and people are often healed. Two weeks ago, for example, the pain in a lady's elbow and arm went! She was so happy! To start with this may need visiting teams or speakers to come and show the way. Sharing of testimonies and stories is critical to building up faith and expectation. There are many rich sources of such stories available on line and in books (see resources section). Though there is nothing like seeing people you know healed and set free!

- **Equipping and activation.** People need to be taught and shown how to pray for the sick, how to receive and give words of knowledge, and experience for themselves the Holy Spirit at work in them.

- **Pastoral care and development of a healing community.** We all need to feel we belong and are encouraged and supported as we learn. However, it is especially important to lovingly address and work through areas of disappointment and fear as the community moves forward.

- **Prayer and spiritual warfare.** We are in a battle; we know who wins the war, but the battle can still be fierce and claim casualties. We need to ensure our churches and leaders have strong intercession cover. As leaders we need to discern spiritual attacks and warfare, and teach and mobilise our churches to pray. Sometimes this also needs fasting, as Jesus taught His disciples.
- **Pursuit of the presence of God.** Ultimately, we as Jesus' followers are 'just' doing as we are told when we pray for people to be healed. It is the Holy Spirit who applies and brings the healing power of Jesus to people. We need to seek Him, His presence, and to be full of the Holy Spirit!

These areas of support for growing in healing actually reflect the operation of the five-fold ministry gifts of Jesus Himself, which is discussed further in chapter 4.

We can also see where churches are by listening to their prayers! I do it to myself sometimes to check where my faith level is at. I have also identified what I believe is likely to be the main issue which needs addressing at each stage. Your reflections on the questions above, however, may lead you to identify other key issues to address.

THEOLOGY	FEAR	KNOW-HOW	UNDERSTANDING AND EXPECTATION	BOLDNESS AND FAITH
God does not heal today (except sovereignly and rarely).	What if people don't get healed?	How do we pray for the sick? Operating in words of knowledge	Building momentum by sharing stories and growing understanding.	Believing for more.
0 **Not for us**	**1** **Dormant**	**2** **Getting going**	**3** **Growing together**	**4** **Thriving body**
I'll pray for strength for you to get through your sickness and learn what the Lord wants to teach you.	Lord, if it's Your will, please heal our friend.	Lord, please heal our friend like we have heard You heal others.	Come, Holy Spirit, to my friend. Be healed in Jesus' name.	Say after me, "Lord Jesus, please heal me." Be healed in Jesus' name. How is it?

WHERE NEXT?

Suggested strategies and supporting resources for each of these stages are given below.

- **Stage 0 and 1:** As church leaders, we need to study the scriptures and seek God. As we are convicted of the truth that God heals today (as I believe we will be!), we need to reconsider our theology and its outworking. It can help to do this through reading books on the subject, watching videos, attending conferences or, for the brave, going on a mission trip. I also recall a challenge from Rick and Bev Murrill, then leaders of Christian Growth International in Chelmsford, England. They basically said that a church's spiritual growth will always be limited by the growth of the leaders. They used the metaphor of eagles soaring – the other eagles could only go as high as the 'leader' eagles. This applies to healing as well as intimacy and spiritual growth. How high are you willing to go?

- **Stage 1 and 2:** As we want to lead our churches out of unbelief or inaction (sometimes provocatively called 'practical atheism'), into seeing healing as a normal part of the Christian life, we can begin to teach on the subject and offer to pray for people. We may want to find church members who are interested and may already be moving in this area and form a ministry team. You may be surprised what 'under the radar' ministry is at work. To really help moving in healing, though, it is often helpful to invite in a visiting speaker, preferably with a team for a service or, better still, a day or weekend. This gives an opportunity for basic teaching, activation, and experience of healing in the body.

One of the biggest obstacles we face is our fear of failure. It's like learning to ice skate. If we spend our time avoiding falling over we hang onto the side and never learn to skate. If we are willing to give it a go and fall over a few times, we will learn much quicker. We need to be like Peter in Matthew 14:22-33 who was willing to jump over the side of the boat and walk on the water! So what if it does 'not work' and we get 'wet', we can trust Jesus. As long as we always act and pray in love we will only learn and bless people.

- **Stage 2 and 3:** To encourage healing ministry to grow in the church further teaching and the development of ministry teams including, for example, healing rooms, can be very helpful. Further external visits or encouragement of members to attend training will help. There are some great training resources available, including video series,[11] and online taught courses. Randy Clark runs three-day and four-day ministry schools in the UK, USA and across many countries on a regular basis.[12]

- **Stage 3 and 4:** Encouraging regular testimonies of healing and opportunities for words of knowledge and healing prayer are important if initial exciting breakthroughs are to become part of the church culture and practice. Testimonies help develop an expectation that God healing people is normative or to be expected, and not unusual. We must keep pressing into God to see the miraculous and see our experience begin to meet the biblical standards we read about. As our churches develop in the healing ministry, we can help share and encourage others too.

The following chapters are designed to help your journey. I hope you find them all helpful!

FOR THOSE IN STAGES 0 AND 1:
- Chapter 3 addresses 'cessationism' and arguments that

---

11 For example, Bill Johnson and Randy Clark's *Essential Guide to Healing* resource pack and the Global Awakening online Certified Christian Healing Practitioner course. https://healingcertification.com/

12 https://globalawakening.com/

healing is not for today. If this is not an issue for you, I suggest you skip the chapter!

- Chapter 4 explores the biblical case for why God heals today, the role of different ministries in helping churches move forwards and some practical tips.

FOR THOSE IN STAGES 1 AND 2:

- Chapter 5 explores fear and disappointment, including my own story of working through the loss of my father.
- Chapters 6 and 7 introduce simple models to pray for the sick and words of knowledge. The Bible study notes in the Appendix/Resources section at the end of the book might be useful here.

FOR THOSE IN STAGES 3 AND 4:

- Chapters 8 and 9 introduce inner healing and deliverance, and key principles for growing in healing ministry.
- The Appendix/Resources section at the end of the book has further resources, including links to messages, websites and contains Bible-study notes for small groups in churches.

THERE IS ALWAYS MORE

I trust this chapter has helped you assess where you are in your journey in the healing ministry. As Paul encourages us in Romans 12:3, '*think of yourself with sober judgment*'. But the challenge now is to press onwards, to see further breakthroughs whether it is into first praying for people to be healed, to seeing the 'first healing', exploring words of knowledge or just releasing more of His love and presence. How will you do this?

We always need to remember it is Jesus who is the healer and has already made it all possible. We 'just' have to believe and act on this! One tip that I have found helpful in the light of this is to get children involved. They usually have not learnt not to believe and trust Jesus! The other Sunday I was praying for someone's foot, which was in a lot of pain. As I prayed a couple of times it got a bit better but I knew the Lord would want to do more. So I asked a young girl of about seven to come and help me. She put her hands on and prayed for healing; I suggested some simple words for her like 'be healed and pain go in Jesus' name'. The pain went, the girl was excited and the person with the foot was happy!

There is a saying: 'Better a wet water walker than a dry boat observer.' Time to get out of the boat, or at least think about it?

3

DOES GOD HEAL TODAY?

"I would rather live in a world where my life is surrounded by mystery than live in a world so small that my mind could comprehend it."

Harry Emerson Fosdick

WHAT WE BELIEVE DETERMINES WHAT WE DO

The battle to restore a basic biblical understanding of healing in most church streams and denominations across the West (it was never really lost elsewhere) has, it seems to me, been largely won. Of course, many churches, especially Pentecostals and parts of the Roman Catholic church, never lost the belief and practice, but for many Protestant churches there has been a big battle to restore it. This is true of the Anglican and Baptist churches I grew up in. I have also come to see how so much of the theology behind the books I read and speakers I listened to (often unwittingly), was influenced by a soft cessationism e.g. a belief that the supernatural activity of the Holy Spirit especially associated with healing has largely stopped.

I remember reading the Bible and wondering why there was such a chasm between the supernatural working of God through

Does God Heal Today?

Jesus and the early church, and our own experience? But it felt as if we didn't really talk about it. When we did ask and search you could find a myriad of reasons. A series of whole arguments had been developed over time usually in reaction to other people's perceived error or excess. This led to the doctrine of 'cessationism', which was notably championed by B.B. Warfield in the USA in the 1800s and still has strong explicit and implicit support.[13]

Dr John Van Rutven has written an excellent, scholarly study on the inherent weakness of Warfield's cessationist position.[14.] He has shown how it is basically inconsistent with its own method of interpreting the Bible and has a fundamentally flawed definition of 'miracle' at its heart. He demonstrates that scripture expects the miraculous, including all the gifts of the Holy Spirit, to continue until the second coming. Critical to this, is the understanding that signs and wonders, including healing, do not merely accredit the gospel during its earliest proclamation, but that these manifestations of the Spirit are an integral part of the gospel, the good news of the Kingdom of God coming.

WHAT DO CESSATIONISTS BELIEVE?

The proponents of this position do not argue that the Holy Spirit is not active in the world today; indeed all Christians would agree that every salvation is a wonderful Spirit-wrought miracle. Nor do they argue that God cannot sovereignly heal

---

13 For example John MacArthur and his 'Strange Fire' conference. https://www.gty.org/library/topical-series-library/325/strange-fire-conference

14 Dr John Van Ruthven, *On the Cessation of the Charismata: The Protestant Polemic on Post-Biblical Miracles.*

today. They tend to focus on the ending of the charismatic gifts of the Spirit at the end of the New Testament or so-called 'Apostolic Era'. For example a respected Professor of Theology, Thomas Schreiner (James Buchanan Harrison professor of New Testament interpretation and associate dean for Scripture and interpretation at The Southern Baptist Theological Seminary in Louisville, Kentucky) states:[15]

> *What about miracles and healings? First, I believe God still heals and does miraculous things today, and we should pray for such. Scripture isn't as clear on this matter, and thus these gifts could exist today. Still, the primary function of these gifts was to accredit the gospel message, confirming that Jesus was both Lord and Christ. I doubt the gift of miracles and healings exists today, for it isn't evident that men and women in our churches have such gifts. Certainly, God can and does heal at times, but where are the people with these gifts? Claims for miracles and healings must be verified, just as the people verified the blind man's healing in John 9. There is a kind of biblically-warranted scepticism.*

Firstly, it is important to note our common ground: 'God still heals and does miraculous things today.' My challenge would be the assertion that the *primary* purpose of gifts was to accredit the message rather than also expressing the coming of the Kingdom and the rule and reign of Jesus as Lord and Christ. Matthew's gospel stresses the ministry of Jesus, as in Matthew

---

15 https://www.thegospelcoalition.org/article/why-i-am-a-cessationist/ accessed 26 /11/17

4 and 9 below, as the proclamation of the Kingdom of God and the healing of all disease. The Kingdom comes with power inherently not just as a helpful illustrative adjunct.

> *Jesus went throughout Galilee, teaching in their synagogues, proclaiming the good news of the kingdom, and healing every disease and illness among the people. News about him spread all over Syria, and people brought to him all who were ill with various diseases, those suffering severe pain, the demon-possessed, those having seizures, and the paralysed; and he healed them. (Matthew 4:23-24)*

> *Jesus went through all the towns and villages, teaching in their synagogues, proclaiming the good news of the kingdom, and healing every disease and illness. (Matthew 9:35)*

As I have described already (and will do elsewhere in this book), I have personally seen such a range of miracles and healings that I believe many, if not most, of these were done by people exercising 'gifts' – God-given gifts based on their identity as children of God and the grace and love of God. Ultimately, miraculous healing is always by God, but I believe He delights to use His children. Many of these miracles are medically attested. I would share the desire of Professor Schreiner and others for continuing to seek and collect evidence. The Global Medical Research Institute is coordinating such efforts.[16]

---

16 https://globalmri.org/

There are four main passages of scripture which have been particularly used to discuss a cessationist or 'continualist' (i.e. the charismatic gifts continue to this day) stance. I will look briefly at each but recommend Dr Ruthven's study for an in-depth exploration of the topic. I will concentrate on the arguments around healing.

PASSAGES FROM 1 CORINTHIANS: WHEN IS COMPLETENESS?

> *I always thank my God for you because of his grace given you in Christ Jesus. For in him you have been enriched in every way – with all kinds of speech and with all knowledge – God thus confirming our testimony about Christ among you. Therefore you do not lack any spiritual gift as you eagerly wait for our Lord Jesus Christ to be revealed. He will also keep you firm to the end, so that you will be blameless on the day of our Lord Jesus Christ. God is faithful, who has called you into fellowship with his Son, Jesus Christ our Lord. (1 Corinthians 1:4-9)*

Paul greets his Christian brothers and sisters in the church he founded in Corinth, with an encouragement to look forward to the coming again of Jesus (the *parousia*). He affirms that Jesus will keep them firm to the end. Meanwhile they 'have been enriched in every way' and 'do not lack any spiritual gift'. This implies the gifts have been given to the Corinthians because they have not yet arrived, as they were in danger of thinking and behaving as so much of Paul's letter goes on to challenge.

Paul is deliberately speaking of an, as yet, not completely realised eschatology. He also stresses that the source of the Corinthian's new-found richness and gifts are the 'grace given' in Jesus Christ.

From this passage we can draw that grace, including gifts, has been given by Jesus to build up, strengthen and prepare God's people for His return. Only then will they be made blameless and there might be no longer a need for all these gifts.

> *Love never fails. But where there are prophecies, they will cease; where there are tongues, they will be stilled; where there is knowledge, it will pass away. For we know in part and we prophesy in part, but when completeness comes, what is in part disappears. When I was a child, I talked like a child, I thought like a child, I reasoned like a child. When I became a man, I put the ways of childhood behind me. For now we see only a reflection as in a mirror; then we shall see face to face. Now I know in part; then I shall know fully, even as I am fully known. And now these three remain: faith, hope and love. But the greatest of these is love. (1 Corinthians 13:8-13)*

The interpretation of verse 10, in particular, is highly contentious! Before exploring it briefly, this passage reminds us of the importance of conducting any discussions with fellow believers we differ with, in love. Love is also the attitude and approach with which we must come to any prayer or healing ministry whatever our beliefs.

This passage appears to argue that in contrast to love, which is eternal and flows from the very nature of God, spiritual gifts are temporary and only characteristic of the present age, until the fullness of Christ's revelation at the second coming (*parousia*).

It is worth reminding ourselves of the overall context of Paul's treatment of spiritual gifts. He emphasises in 1 Corinthians 12 above that gifts are given by Christ for service to many for the common good. They are not to accredit people, confer status or puff the recipient up. Rather their purpose is to build up one body from many diverse gifts.

> *There are different kinds of gifts, but the same Spirit distributes them. There are different kinds of service, but the same Lord. There are different kinds of working, but in all of them and in everyone it is the same God at work. Now to each one the manifestation of the Spirit is given for the common good. To one there is given through the Spirit a message of wisdom, to another a message of knowledge by means of the same Spirit, to another faith by the same Spirit, to another gifts of healing by that one Spirit, to another miraculous powers, to another prophecy, to another distinguishing between spirits, to another speaking in different kinds of tongues, and to still another the interpretation of tongues. All these are the work of one and the same Spirit, and he distributes them to each one, just as he determines. (1 Corinthians 12:4-11)*

The question of contention then in 1 Corinthians 13 is that if love is eternal, how long do the gifts last for? When is '*but when completeness comes*' in verse 10? Essentially are they until the second coming, the *parousia*, of Christ as set out in the discussion around 1 Corinthians 1 or did they cease at the end of the apostolic era i.e. when the last 'first-hand eyewitness' of Christ died or at the completion of the New Testament canon? The latter was finally agreed in AD 382 at the Council of Rome though most of the twenty-seven books were identified by the time of Origen in the third century, if not earlier. From my reading of the arguments I believe a good case can be made for the *parousia*. The Greek word *telion* translated as 'completeness' appears to fit with 1 Corinthians 1:8 as discussed above. A recent study has also shown the Early Church Fathers clearly understood the word as relating to the *parousia*.[17]

The exact meaning of the grammatical construction of verse 10 is contested but it would appear to imply that gifts cease '*when* completeness comes' i.e. not before but at the point of completeness, the *parousia*. The illustrations Paul uses in verse 11 and 12 of maturity to adulthood and of seeing an image in a mirror, and his statement, '*Now I know in part; then I shall know fully, even as I am fully known*' point again to an event yet to come.

Thus, I would argue that Paul is looking forward to Christ's return as the moment we will be made 'complete' or 'perfect' as it is put in other translations. Meanwhile the gifts, including healing and miracles (and other 'charismatic' gifts), are given by Christ for service to many believers within the church for the common good. Rather their purpose is to build up one body from many diverse gifts to continue Christ's working of announcing and demonstrating the Kingdom of God.

---

17 Dr John Van Ruthven, *On the Cessation of the Charismata: The Protestant Polemic on Post-Biblical Miracles*, pp 126 ff.

Sophia, wisdom, by Rebecca Jesty

DOES EARLY CHURCH HISTORY BACK UP THE CESSATION OF HEALING?

Much of the cessationist argument around such verses seems to then rely on an understanding of church history that the miraculous and gifts of healing stopped around the end of the 'apostolic era'. However, this does not appear to be the case. For example, Justin Martyr (100-165, martyred in AD 165) wrote in his 'apology' addressed to the Roman emperor:

"For numberless demoniacs throughout the whole world, and in your city, many of our Christian men exorcising them in the name of Jesus Christ . . . have healed and do heal, rendering helpless and driving the possessing devils out of the men, though they could not be cured by all the other exorcists, and those who used incantations and drug."

Justin Martyr tells in several places how Christians healed in the name of Jesus Christ, driving out demons and all kinds of evil spirits. Writing about the charismata, the gifts God pours out upon believers, he calls attention to the power to heal as one of the particular gifts that was being received and used.[18]

Many other Early Church Fathers and 'Doctors' also wrote about their personal experience of carrying out and witnessing healing and deliverance, including Tertullian, Origen, Irenaeus, Athanasius, Gregory of Nazianzus, and Basil the Great to name but a few. Indeed, Augustine himself attested to and practised healing in the last few years of his ministry despite his popularised theology on the 'blueprint view' which so undermined expectations

---

18 Quoted from *Empowered Workbook* by Dr Randy Clark (Global Awakening, 2011).

Does God Heal Today?

and practice around healing in the centuries which followed.[19]

The story of why healing and deliverance did not seem to continue to consistently be reported through church history is complex. It is a mixture of theology developing to explain suffering and so the focus was there as in Augustine's 'blueprint' worldview e.g. everything that happens is set out for us by God, so our work is to learn from it and grow. This is in contrast to the previous, and I would argue, New Testament 'warfare' view. The latter sees the Kingdom of God advancing against the kingdom of darkness. A war where we know the winner, but the battles still must be fought – and even are sometimes lost. In the 'blueprint' worldview, the focus becomes the absence of healing and not what increases it. In addition, social, political, and cultural factors contributed as well as a tendency to react against everything others stood for rather than identifying the good and bad, and keeping the good. Kelsey and Clark in the references discuss this further but I would argue this is not a reason to argue for the cessation of gifts as the intention or will of God.

As to whether healing continues today I would encourage any 'biblically sceptical' fellow believer to come and see! There are many online links or books or, better still, come to a meeting or a mission trip. For me one hour of experience effectively undid fifty years of 'faulty' teaching and lowered expectation.

THE GIFT OF APOSTLES?

Another major plank of cessationist argument is around the

---

19 See *Empowered Workbook* by Dr Randy Clark, and Morton T. Kelsey, *Healing and Christianity* (New York, NY: Harper and Row Publishers, 1973, 1976).

ending of the offices of apostles and prophets at the end of the apostolic era. This is variously cited as when the last 'firsthand eyewitness' of Christ died or at the completion of the New Testament canon. This is because miracles of healing and others are seen by cessationists as primarily attesting to the credibility of the miracle worker as the speaker and bringer of truth. They would point to passages around Moses (for example, Exodus 4:1-5 below), Elisha and Elijah, Jesus, and the apostles.

> *Moses answered, 'What if they do not believe me or listen to me and say, "The Lord did not appear to you"?' Then the Lord said to him, 'What is that in your hand?' 'A staff,' he replied. The Lord said, 'Throw it on the ground.' Moses threw it on the ground and it became a snake, and he ran from it. Then the Lord said to him, 'Reach out your hand and take it by the tail.' So Moses reached out and took hold of the snake and it turned back into a staff in his hand. 'This,' said the Lord, 'is so that they may believe that the Lord, the God of their fathers – the God of Abraham, the God of Isaac and the God of Jacob – has appeared to you.'*

The argument[20] is that 'In thousands of years of human history, there were only about two hundred years in which God empowered men to work miracles. And even during those years, miracles were not common, everyday event' and that 'God's primary purpose in giving men (sic) power to work miracles was to validate them as His messengers'.

---

20 Tom Pennington, Pastor-Teacher at Countryside Bible Church in Southlake, Texas and speaker at Strange Fire. https://www.gty.org/library/blog/B140505

Does God Heal Today?

Whilst it is clear that the working of miracles and healings was used to attest to these men speaking truth, this does not confine the miracles and healings to this alone. There are many miracles and healings cited without proclamation of the truth or salvation being recorded. As stated above, I would argue the miracles and healings are overt demonstrations of the reality and inherent nature of the Kingdom of God, not just 'signposts' or 'certificates of truth'. This is consistent with the New Testament believers in Corinth, Rome and other churches receiving spiritual gifts that included miracle-working and healing. As discussed above there is no sense in Paul's letters that these are time limited.

If this is accepted then the distinction between 'eyewitness apostles' and any subsequent apostles appears less critical to the argument. There appear to be people acting in an apostolic capacity in the New Testament who do not appear to be part of Jesus' immediate band of disciples or 'eyewitnesses' of Jesus. These include Timothy, Silvanus, Andronicus and Junia (from Romans 16:7, see below), Barnabas, Apollos, and Epaphroditus.

Greet Andronicus and Junia, my fellow Jews who have been in prison with me. They are outstanding among the apostles, and they were in Christ before I was.

I would recognise the roles of 'apostles' and the 'apostolic' gifts as a key feature of church growth and indeed movements of God around the world and through church history from

John Wesley to Heidi and Rolland Baker.[21] Obviously these apostles have not been eyewitnesses of Jesus on the earth but have often had significant personal encounters with Jesus and the Holy Spirit. The apostolic ministry seeks to 'bring heaven down to earth'. It focuses on establishing the culture and presence of heaven and the kingdom of God. This can be expressed, for example, through church planting and/or cultural transformation.

Similarly, I would recognise the role of prophets and prophetic gifts to 'translate God' for people,[22] groups, and wider society in the moment, drawing people to His ways and will. Prophecy today must always be consistent with biblical truth and will often directly apply it. It is not to set out new truth at variance with the nature of God and His plans revealed in the Bible, His written word, but brings life and hope as the *rhema* or 'living now word'.

Consequently, you are no longer foreigners and strangers, but fellow citizens with God's people and also members of his household, built on the foundation of the apostles and prophets, with Christ Jesus himself as the chief cornerstone. (Ephesians 2:19-20)

So, when Paul writes to the Ephesian church of their 'foundation of the apostles and prophets' (in 2:20) it is not inconsistent with his statement of Christ giving further ministry giftings to the church in 4:11. These are to equip the members of His

---

21 *Defining Moments*, Bill Johnson and Jennifer Miskov (Whitaker House, 2016).

22 As described by Shawn Bolz in his book of the same name.

church, so the church might become united and mature – with the fullness of Christ.

> *But to each one of us grace has been given as Christ apportioned it. This is why it says: 'When he ascended on high, he took many captives and gave gifts to his people.' (What does 'he ascended' mean except that he also descended to the lower, earthly region? He who descended is the very one who ascended higher than all the heavens, in order to fill the whole universe.) So Christ himself gave the apostles, the prophets, the evangelists, the pastors and teachers, to equip his people for works of service, so that the body of Christ may be built up until we all reach unity in the faith and in the knowledge of the Son of God and become mature, attaining to the whole measure of the fullness of Christ. (Ephesians 4:7-13)*

This does not appear to have yet happened and thus these ministries are still needed. They will be, I would suggest, until Jesus returns.

Furthermore, in this list are *'the apostles, the prophets, the evangelists, the pastors and teachers'*. There is no sense in the text that the ministries (and offices) of apostles and prophets might cease but evangelists, teachers and pastors continue, as all mainline Christian denominations would accept.

I believe that apostolic and prophetic ministries, giftings and associated mindsets, are essential for a healthy church. Their role alongside the other Ascension gifts of Jesus, also called the 'Ephesians 4' or five-fold ministries, is to equip and raise up believers in the full range of biblical ministry and gifts including healing. This is explored further in the next chapter.

Alan Hirsch helpfully says, "One of the most clarifying definitions of ministry then, is doing the kind of things that Jesus did for the same reason that He did them."[23]

BE TRANSFORMED BY THE RENEWING OF YOUR MIND

This chapter has explored the arguments around healing for today. As I have argued, I believe healing ministry is an essential part of the calling and commission of today's church. Understanding and walking this out might require considerable renewal of your thinking, as I found.

This can be a progressive process as we seek the Lord, study the scriptures and let Him teach us from experience. For example, I had heard teaching about how you can be healed by just hearing a word, a *rhema* word, and not even need prayer. I read it in the Bible, heard this taught, and saw people healed like this. This built up my understanding and belief so that I taught this myself. And then a few weeks ago, I saw someone healed 'just' by 'receiving' a word I felt God wanted to share about His desire to heal people with elbow pain.

What we believe determines how we think and what we do. In what ways around healing do you think your mind needs to be renewed?

---

23 Alan Hirsch, *The Forgotten Ways*

4

RESTORING BIBLICAL BELIEF AND PRACTICE

"The great Christian revolutions came not by the discovery of something that was not known before. They happen when someone takes radically something that was always there."

H. Richard Niebuhr

John Wimber, Francis MacNutt, Dr Randy Clark, Bill Johnson, Derek Prince, Ian Andrews, and Peter Horrobin, amongst many others, have helped enormously to restore the healing and deliverance ministries to mainstream thinking. However, I don't, as yet, see healing restored to mainstream practice such that most churches expect to see supernatural healing as regular and not rare.

The challenge today is that many church leaders and members have grown up subtly influenced by soft cessationism. I was shocked by how many of the writers I had read as a young Christian, and the books on theology I had read which basically came from this school. So, we have churches full of what Randy Clark calls 'unbelieving believers'. This is the challenge of stage 0 or 'dormant' churches, as I have called them.

Today the sheer weight of evidence for supernatural signs and wonders, including healing, is enormous, especially in the explosive growth of churches in Latin America, Africa, and Asia. The story of Heidi and Rolland Baker in Mozambique is one example of many.[24] On the back of healings, and even resurrections from the dead, their movement has planted over ten thousand churches. Increasingly, we are seeing the same impact in the West. For example, the church in Wales under the auspices of New Wine Wales, is seeing thousands of people healed.[25] In Budapest the 'Felhaz' movement amongst students has grown from three to thousands in a little over two years, based on the supernatural gifts at work in an exciting move of God. In my own church and ministry, I have seen over a hundred healings this year alone. Healing has become regular. Not always, not guaranteed, but regular.

WHY DOES GOD HEAL TODAY?

There are many reasons why God heals, in which we can root our faith and action. I have listed some below based on biblical references. However, all essentially flow out of the loving nature of God Himself and His desire to see people, made in His image, reconciled to Him, and restored to wholeness. Healing is not just a demonstration of His love and power; it is intrinsic to His nature and character. He is the Healer-God, the One who seeks the reconciliation and restoration of all people and all creation. Nowhere was this better demonstrated than in Jesus' life and ministry. Jesus, who said He only did what He saw the Father doing. Ultimately once the 'war' is

---

24 See http://www.irisglobal.org/ and books or videos such as *Compelled by Love* by Heidi Baker (Charisma House, 2008).

25 See Appendix/Resources section for link to a talk by Julian Richards, leader of New Wine Wales.

over and all evil and its consequences are destroyed, John in Revelation 21 tells us that God will make His dwelling with man and all sickness, illness, pain, and suffering will have ended. As the Bible makes clear, we as men and women also have to choose to dwell with Him too, to accept His *sozo* offer of new life: salvation, healing, and deliverance.

> *Then I saw 'a new heaven and a new earth,' for the first heaven and the first earth had passed away, and there was no longer any sea. I saw the Holy City, the new Jerusalem, coming down out of heaven from God, prepared as a bride beautifully dressed for her husband. And I heard a loud voice from the throne saying, 'Look! God's dwelling-place is now among the people, and he will dwell with them. They will be his people, and God himself will be with them and be their God. "He will wipe every tear from their eyes. There will be no more death" or mourning or crying or pain, for the old order of things has passed away.' (Revelation 21:1-4)*

Until then, however, we are called and commissioned, i.e. Jesus has given us 'orders' and equipped us by the Holy Spirit, to heal people and deliver them from evil spirits to demonstrate this kingdom has come and is coming.

The biblical illustrations include the following:

- His nature and character as a loving Father who revealed Himself as 'Jehova-Rappha', the God the healer (Exodus 15:26):

He said, 'If you listen carefully to the LORD your God and do what is right in his eyes, if you pay attention to his commands and keep all his decrees, I will not bring on you any of the diseases I brought on the Egyptians, for I am the LORD, who heals you.'

- The prophetic purpose of Jesus as Messiah, in His death and resurrection (Isaiah 53:4-5), which is quoted in Matthew 8:14-17.

When Jesus came into Peter's house, he saw Peter's mother-in-law lying in bed with a fever. He touched her hand and the fever left her, and she got up and began to wait on him. When evening came, many who were demon-possessed were brought to him, and he drove out the spirits with a word and healed all who were ill. This was to fulfil what was spoken through the prophet Isaiah: 'He took up our infirmities and bore our diseases.'

- The Kingdom of God as inaugurated by Jesus.

Jesus went throughout Galilee, teaching in their synagogues, proclaiming the good news of the kingdom, and healing every disease and illness among the people. News about him spread all over Syria, and people brought to him all who were ill with various diseases, those suffering severe pain, the demon-possessed, those having seizures, and the paralysed; and he healed them. (Matthew 4:23-24)

Jesus went through all the towns and villages, teaching in their synagogues, proclaiming the good news of the kingdom, and healing every disease and illness. (Matthew 9:35)

- The commission of Jesus to His disciples.

When Jesus had called the Twelve together, he gave them power and authority to drive out all demons and to cure diseases, and he sent them out to proclaim the kingdom of God and to heal those who were ill. (Luke 9:1-2)

After this the Lord appointed seventy-two others and sent them two by two ahead of him to every town and place where he was about to go. He told them, 'The harvest is plentiful, but the workers are few. Ask the Lord of the harvest, therefore, to send out workers into his harvest field. Go! I am sending you out like lambs among wolves. Do not take a purse or bag or sandals; and do not greet anyone on the road . . . Heal those who are ill and tell them, "The kingdom of God has come near to you."' (Luke 10:1-4, 9)

- Compassion and love of Jesus – we see this so much but one of the most touching stories is where Jesus interrupts a funeral. So this is a resurrection, not 'just' a healing. The same love, compassion and power are demonstrated.

Soon afterwards, Jesus went to a town called Nain, and his disciples and a large crowd went along with him. As he approached the town gate, a dead person was being carried out – the only son of his mother, and she was a widow. And a large crowd from the town was with her. When the Lord saw her, his heart went out to her and he said, 'Don't cry.' Then he went up and touched the bier they were carrying him on, and the bearers stood still. He said, 'Young man, I say to you, get up!' The dead man sat up and began to talk, and Jesus gave him back to his mother. They were all filled with awe and praised God. 'A great prophet has appeared among us,' they said. 'God has come to help his people.' This news about Jesus spread throughout Judea and the surrounding country. (Luke 7:11-17)

- Demonstration of the defeat of Satan.

If it is by the Spirit of God that I drive out demons, then the kingdom of God has come upon you. (Matthew 12:28)

- Demonstrate the works and glory of God.

As he went along, he saw a man blind from birth. His disciples asked him, 'Rabbi, who sinned, this man or his parents, that he was born blind?' 'Neither this man nor his parents sinned,' said Jesus, 'but this happened so that the works of God might be displayed in him. As long as it is day, we must do the works of him who sent me. Night is coming, when no one can work. While I am in the world, I am the light of the world.' After saying this, he spat on the ground, made some mud with the saliva, and put it on the man's eyes. 'Go' he told him, 'wash in the Pool of Siloam' (this word means 'Sent'). So the man went and washed, and came home seeing. (John 9:1-7)

- Faith: people understand the nature and heart of the Lord and trust in Him as the centurion did to Jesus' amazement in Luke 7.

When Jesus had finished saying all this to the people who were listening, he entered Capernaum. There a centurion's servant, whom his master valued highly, was ill and about to die. The centurion heard of Jesus and sent some elders of the Jews to him, asking him to come and heal his servant. When they came to Jesus, they pleaded earnestly with him, 'This man deserves to have you do this, because he loves our nation and has built our synagogue. So Jesus went with them. He was not far from the house when the centurion sent friends to say to him: 'Lord, don't trouble yourself, for I do not deserve to have you come under my roof. That is why I did not even consider myself worthy to come to you. But say the word, and my servant will be healed. For I myself am a man under authority, with soldiers under me. I tell this one, 'Go', and he goes; and that one, 'Come', and he comes. I say to my servant, 'Do this', and he does it.' When Jesus heard this, he was amazed at him, and turning to the crowd following him, he said, 'I tell you, I have not found such great faith even in Israel.' Then the men who had been sent returned to the house and found the servant well. (Luke 7:1-10)

- Outworking of our relationship with Jesus as children of God and co-heirs with Him.

Very truly I tell you, whoever believes in me will do the works I have been doing, and they will do even greater things than these, because I am going to the Father. (John 14:12)

- Operation of the gifts of the Holy Spirit including healing, miracles, and faith (1 Corinthians 12).

There are different kinds of gifts, but the same Spirit distributes them. There are different kinds of service, but the same Lord. There are different kinds of working, but in all of them and in everyone it is the same God at work. Now to each one the manifestation of the Spirit is given for the common good. To one there is given through the Spirit a message of wisdom, to another a message of knowledge by means of the same Spirit, to another faith by the same Spirit, to another gifts of healing by that one Spirit, to another miraculous powers, to another prophecy, to another distinguishing between spirits, to another speaking in different kinds of tongues, and to still another the interpretation of tongues. All these are the work of one and the same Spirit, and he distributes them to each one, just as he determines. (1 Corinthians 12:4-11)

JESUS-LIKE CHURCH: THE FIVE-FOLD EPHESIANS 4 MINISTRIES

So if we are clear that God as Father, Son and Holy Spirit, does heal today, our next task is to consider how He uses His body, the church, to do this. This is where we return to the five-fold ministry pattern and gifts of Jesus that Paul outlines in Ephesians 4.

I believe that apostolic and prophetic ministries, giftings and associated mindsets, are essential for a healthy church. Their role alongside the other Ascension gifts of Jesus, also called the 'Ephesians 4' or five-fold ministries, is to equip and raise up believers in the full range of biblical ministry and gifts including healing. All these ministries have key roles to play in developing and sustaining a balanced healing ministry. These five-fold functions and ministries are rooted in Jesus Himself and His own ministry. According to Alan Hirsch, they are key to Christ's body, the church, maturing and reflecting the fullness of Christ.[26]

Apostles – seek the presence of God and to bring heaven to earth, establishing the appropriate culture and expression for the body of Christ to thrive in, within a particular cultural context. Individuals called as apostles are often associated with healing, signs, and wonders. For instance, in the 1970s and 80s, John Wimber had a huge impact on regaining the expectation in the church that 'ordinary believers' could pray for healing. His ministry, solidly based on theology and teaching, helped usher in what Peter Wagner called 'The Third Wave of the Holy Spirit'. Randy Clark, John Arnott, Bill Johnson and others have built on this and extended our understanding and practice.

Prophets – help birth and grow a deepening hunger for intimacy and the presence of God in believers which is critical to going deeper in healing. They also encourage and equip believers to

---

26 5Q: *Reactivating the Original Intelligence and Capacity of the Body of Christ* by Alan Hirsch (100 Movements, 2017).

hear from the Lord themselves, to 'translate God'[27] bringing truth and hope to people. The prophetic word in the moment (*rhema*) whether it is a biblical quote, application or a word of love, truth and hope (always consistent with the Bible) can also release healing. It is closely aligned to 'words of knowledge', described further in chapter 8.

Evangelists – encourage and equip believers to share God's love with people, overcoming fear and indifference. Healing and other supernatural gifts can play a major role in leading people to Christ. As in Acts 13:12, when Paul blinded the local sorcerer.

When the proconsul saw what had happened, he believed, for he was amazed at the teaching about the Lord.

Craig S. Keener, a professor of New Testament at Asbury Theological Seminary[28] reported that 'in many countries, healing is the main reason for the explosion of charismatic/Pentecostal – and Christian – growth rates. As of about ten years ago, it was estimated that perhaps half of all conversions to Christianity were because of experiences with healing.'

Pastors – training, encouraging, and motivating believers to care for each other. The pastoral urge to love, care for, and help people needs to be expressed in how healing is offered and exercised. Pastoral sensitivity and wisdom is needed in many

---

27 As described by Shawn Bolz in his book of the same name.

28 Quoted in https://www.charismamag.com/spirit/supernatural/22492-the-healing-miracles-preacher

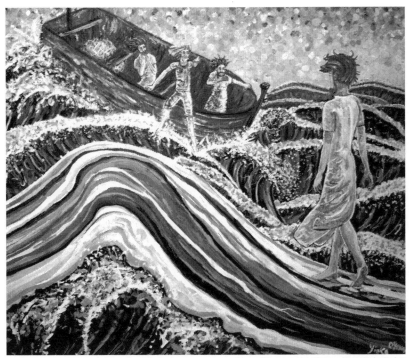

Peter walking on water with Jesus, by Rev Yinka Oyekan

difficult situations such as where people are near death, mentally ill, have learning difficulties, have complex multi-factorial problems or have had bad experiences with healing before. However, my personal experience and belief is we should not let pastoral concern blot out bold faith. We need both, like Jesus!

Teachers – believers need to be taught a strong biblical foundation for healing and deliverance, both for their own health and for ministry to others. Truth can set us free and modern neuroscience has shown that changing our thinking can bring healing in itself, as the Bible has always taught us!

LEADING OUR CHURCHES INTO HEALING

In the chapters ahead we will explore in more detail how we can lead our churches into growing in ministering healing. Here are some initial practical considerations for leaders.

- Teach and lay the biblical ground and expectation for healing and illustrate this with testimony and stories. These can be from your own experiences, from congregation members or using videos and stories from trusted sources (see resources section). There are historical examples in every denomination and church stream to draw from.
- And when you teach, don't be afraid to try out getting people to pray for those needing healing! Randy Clark encourages people to acknowledge when there has been an eighty per cent improvement, recognising that there

is often a process in healing. We might ask people to wave their arms above their heads or clap. This helps build faith.

- There are many ways to offer opportunities for healing regularly within the church setting: consider what works best for your church tradition, style and history. Examples include:
  - » dedicated healing services,
  - » developing ministry teams offering prayer at the end of services,
  - » including prayer for healing within services, especially around communion,
  - » dedicated healing sessions.
- There are various approaches that also offer prayer for non-church members and even reach out specifically to not-yet-believers:
  - » healing rooms,[29]
  - » healing cafes,[30]
  - » spirit cafes (which concentrate more on prophecy and inner healing),[31]
  - » healing on the streets,[32]
  - » offer prayer as part of outreach including through street evangelism and The Turning. We have seen an increasing number of people receive physical healing

---

29 The International Association of Healing Rooms is based on the original multi-church Spokane model, http://www.healingrooms.org.uk/. Other churches including The Gate have developed their healing rooms based on Bethel's model – see http://bethelredding.com/content/healing-rooms

30 See New Wine Wales, http://newwinecymru.co.uk/healing-homepage/healing-cafes/

31 See Lori Arnott and Harvest ministries: http://www.harvestministries.co.uk/spirit-cafe-training/4590449432

32 https://www.healingonthestreets.com/

when we've met them on the streets. I recall a young lad outside the job centre in Cardiff who was happy to pray to invite Jesus into his life. I realised he had a painful hand which came from a burn at work. Using the approach outlined in chapter 7, I prayed twice for him, and all the pain went! Healing can really help people experience God's love and open them up to inviting Jesus into their lives.

- Ensure opportunities for testimonies and stories on a regular basis to help build faith and expectation. As Revelation 19:10b in NKJV states: '*For the testimony of Jesus is the spirit of prophecy.*'
- Consider bringing in an outside speaker or team to teach and activate the congregation initially and/or to encourage growth.
- Encourage people to experience healing in different contexts e.g. on mission trips or at conferences. 'Escaping' the constraints of Western Christianity can be very powerful in exposure to the supernatural, as my own story illustrates.
- Sensitively address issues around unanswered prayer and pastoral issues on individual and, as needed, a corporate basis. As discussed in previous chapters, if we don't tackle these issues they can hold people back in fear and disappointment.

ROOTED AND ESTABLISHED
The scriptures in this chapter encourage and root us in the

biblical rationale for healing. You need to develop deep roots in biblical understanding and relationship with Jesus to press into the healing ministry. Whilst I believe you will see amazing victories and healing, you are likely to experience failures and disappointments, which we will explore in the next chapter.

Last week I prayed for three people in the workplace. Only one was healed: and in a GP surgery! As I was waiting for the doctor I was meeting to kindly make me a cup of tea, the person told me they had hurt their hand and couldn't type properly. I asked if I could pray for them; they were happy for me to pray though I don't think they have any faith as yet. When I came back from the meeting, they told me their hand was much better! They even emailed me the next day to say it was still better! The other two, however, weren't healed. One had a really painful toe that didn't respond to prayer. I even managed to stand on it later. So a mixed week but our experience shouldn't shape our practice.

Ultimately our healing ministry must flow from our relationship with God as His dearly loved and precious children. He alone is the source of our power and authority to heal. But He has commanded you and me to pray for the sick so we can trust Him to back up His command and word!

5

OVERCOMING FEAR: DEALING WITH DISAPPOINTMENT

"Treasure the questions as they rage in my mind
I treasure the questions some day I will find
You see I ran out of answers such a long time ago
And I treasure the questions wherever I go"

(Written by Martyn Joseph)

THE ELEPHANT IN THE ROOM

One of the major reasons I find that believers, and especially leaders, don't press into healing is that they have either experienced disappointment, or fear arousing it in others. I think this is often the main challenge of stage 1 in activating a church in healing.

In all honesty, disappointment is inevitable in the healing ministry. It's an issue we must face and be ready to help church members work through it. Otherwise they will join the many Christians who have accepted that the gifts of the Holy Spirit are for today, but do not step out in healing. So many are held in inactivity because they have either already suffered discouragement or fear it.

Often church leaders, their denominations, and individual believers, have developed a 'theology' to explain why they don't practise healing. Somehow, when pressed, they must explain how their experience does not match scripture and the accounts of Jesus' life, ministry, and commissioning of His disciples. Underlying these issues is often the real fear of what happens when people are not healed. What about those who have not been healed? How will they feel? Why does no one get healed when I pray? What about those we loved dearly, and prayed passionately for, yet were not healed, or even died?

MY STRUGGLE: WHAT TO DO IN THE FACE OF DEATH?

I have already related how, for many years, I would pray for people but never ask them if anything had happened lest I find out nothing had happened! That would feel awkward. Best avoided.

I learnt, however, from the teaching of Dr Randy Clark, and others, that asking what was happening was an essential and sensible step, based on Jesus' own practice. So, I grew in my understanding, and practice of healing, especially on a mission trip to Brazil. I resolved to see in my home church and country what I saw in Brazil.

After the initial excitement at church where we saw many folks healed, I entered a real testing period. Two particular people stand out.

An old school friend's wife, Sarah, had been battling leukaemia for four years. She wrote some amazingly inspiring blogs and

Overcoming Fear: Dealing with Disappointment

posts through which her faith shone. People in over seventy-five countries received these. Many no doubt were praying, but she got worse. I felt prompted to go and pray for her. By now it was Christmas 2014 and she was in a hospice. I will never forget going to see her on Boxing Day and praying for her alongside her husband and brother-in-law. I was full of faith as I knew the Lord had prompted me to go. She was unconscious: just skin and bone. As we prayed the Holy Spirit was very evidently 'all over her'. Yet she did not recover and died later that day.

She was the same age as I was and was also the beloved mother of three children. The funeral was full of rejoicing at a life marvellously lived, but full of pain at one cut short way too soon. I was left asking, 'What was that all about, Lord?' I remember deciding to put the experience in the 'mystery box' and keep believing and praying for healing.

It was then my greatest test to date. My father had been diagnosed with prostate cancer some years ago and had opted, with his consultant's support and guidance, for conservative treatment. Alas he was one of the less than half per cent of prostate patients in whom a further, or secondary cancer grows. He then battled the disease for about four years. We prayed and prayed. I did all I (then) knew by way of dealing with other related issues (see later chapters). By January 2015, just after Sarah died, his condition worsened such that I had to drive him to the Royal Marsden Hospital one Sunday afternoon.

He never came home.

After a few weeks of ups and downs, it became obvious his treatment was not working. I had a very painful conversation with a doctor on the phone one Sunday. Dad had opted not to continue active treatment. He was ready to die. Going to see him and saying that we, I, released him to die was incredibly painful, and emotionally tough. He then lasted four more weeks. During this time, we could talk and joke, and say all those things you really want your loved ones to hear.

He was ready to die; he did get fed up with the process of dying – but he knew where, and to Whom he was going. Steady streams of visitors came to see him and were comforted. He died, and we gave thanks for a wonderful father, husband, grandfather, community activist, and peacemaker. He had lived a good life and was eighty-two years old. But there is a whole family, set of friends, and community who still needed him.

I still miss him, but even as I gave the address at his funeral, I was determined to keep believing for, and praying for healing. My God was, is, and always will be, whatever I feel, think, or say, bigger than any questions, disappointment, pain, or fears I may have. In my tears, it was another one for the 'mystery box'.

Even today, at our church, as we have preached and taught on healing over six months, and seen many healed, the mystery box is needed every week. Right in the front row in her wheelchair sits the amazing Ann. Ann (at the time of writing) has MS and has very limited movement. Yet, every week, she is up for prayer. Every week she would have us keep pressing in for more.

There are many others with long-term conditions such as strokes, diabetes, and MS who also would have us keep pressing in. Even if they have not been healed yet. I think this is only possible if we truly love each other, and if we are honest about the pain and disappointment.

More recently the church has seen one of our most encouraging, amazing, and faith-filled members die after a brief but tenacious and brave fight against secondary cancer. Julia was the leader of our church intercession team. She had pressed in for healing, even declaring that our church will become a cancer-free zone. Yet despite much prayer she died. Father has received her into His presence, where I am sure she continues to pray for our church. Why did she die? We don't know. We can only grieve together, rejoicing for her life and faithful witness, and loving and supporting her family.

Jesus also knew pain and loss in His earthly life. Matthew 14:6-14 records the death of His cousin and perhaps one of the very few people who really knew who He, Jesus, was. John the Baptist died a seemingly pointless death at the hands of a capricious king and his manipulative wife.

On Herod's birthday the daughter of Herodias danced for the guests and pleased Herod so much that he promised with an oath to give her whatever she asked. Prompted by her mother, she said, 'Give me here on a dish the head of John the Baptist.' The king was distressed, but because of his oaths and his dinner guests, he ordered that her request be granted and had John beheaded in the prison. His head was brought in on a dish and

*given to the girl, who carried it to her mother. John's disciples
came and took his body and buried it. Then they went and told
Jesus. When Jesus heard what had happened, he withdrew by
boat privately to a solitary place. Hearing of this, the crowds
followed him on foot from the towns. When Jesus landed and
saw a large crowd, he had compassion on them and healed
those who were ill.*

Jesus was obviously impacted by John's death and sought solitude
with His Father. The next section will describe a suggested
process for such times.

In His time with His Father, Jesus would have had to process
His pain, receive His Father's love and affirmation, and reconfirm
His commitment to His mission. We see this because
immediately He is thrust back into ministry as crowds swarm
around Him. He has the emotional and spiritual resources to
have 'compassion on them' and He 'healed those who were ill'.
Even as I write these words, I can hear Julia, and others who
have died prematurely despite faith-filled prayer, urging us to
go and do likewise. Love those in front of us and heal them!

As Job said to his friends in Job 13:15, *'Though he slay me,
yet will I hope in him.'*

As the brave young Hebrew refugees, Shadrach, Meshach and
Abednego, said to the king who held their lives in his hands,
in Daniel 3:16-18 (emphasis added):

*'King Nebuchadnezzar, we do not need to defend ourselves
before you in this matter. If we are thrown into the blazing*

WE ALL GET TO PLAY

Overcoming Fear: Dealing with Disappointment

*furnace, the God we serve is able to deliver us from it, and he will deliver us from Your Majesty's hand. **But even if he does not**, we want you to know, Your Majesty, that we will not serve your gods or worship the image of gold you have set up.'*

We need to exercise faith to see God heal and work miracles. But we need a deeper faith that endures and trusts when we do not see healing, when our fervent prayers are unanswered, and our hearts ache with pain and grief. Pete Greig, founder of the amazing 24-7 prayer movement, has written a powerful and very helpful book on unanswered prayer: *God on Mute*[33] exploring this further. He quotes some graffiti found on the wall of a house in Kohn, Germany in 1945 where a Jewish believer was hiding from the Gestapo:

I believe in the sun even when it isn't shining.
I believe in love even when I am alone.
I believe in God even when He is silent.

Disappointment and pain is inevitable. It can come from many sources. It can be from apparently unanswered prayer, especially when people die or go on living in desperate situations. Conversely it can be from when we fail to respond to the Lord's prompt, and 'duck' an opportunity. Our disappointment can be in ourselves, in others, or in God. I think that pain, and disappointment, is inevitable in life and in the healing ministry. The key is how we respond.

---

33 Pete Greig, *God on Mute* (David C. Cook, 2007).

DEALING WITH DISAPPOINTMENT

Above all else, guard your heart, for it is the wellspring of life.
(Proverbs 4:23)[34]

Key to avoiding disappointment derailing us in healing and, indeed more significantly, our walk with the Lord is what happens in our hearts. The writer of Proverbs says that 'above all' i.e. it is of prime importance that we guard our hearts. To guard implies that we both watch over and monitor our hearts – what's going on, what we are feeling and how we are reacting as well as protecting what comes in. 'Heart' speaks of our mind, our thoughts, and feelings in our innermost being. The writer says the 'heart' is critical as it is the 'wellspring' or source of all I do. Jesus referred to our hearts in this way in Mark:

> And then he added, 'It is what comes from inside that defiles you. For from within, out of a person's heart, come evil thoughts, sexual immorality, theft, murder, adultery, greed, wickedness, deceit, lustful desires, envy, slander, pride, and foolishness. All these vile things come from within; they are what defile you.'
> (Mark 7:20-23 NLT)

Whatever testing, pain, and disappointment we go through, we need 'soft hearts'. We need to not take offence at others or even at the Lord. Paul urges us to deal promptly with our issues and so avoid letting the devil get a 'legal right' to affect us.

---

34 NIV 1984 Edition.

Overcoming Fear: Dealing with Disappointment

'In your anger do not sin': do not let the sun go down while you are still angry, and do not give the devil a foothold. (Ephesians 4:26-27)

David knew what it was to have such a soft heart, even after his own sin and disobedience.

My sacrifice, O God, is a broken spirit; a broken and contrite heart you, God, will not despise. (Psalm 51:17)

But the truth is it hurts. It can really, really hurt and grieve us deep in our souls. It can cause us to question ourselves, our calling and even God's love and character. If we do not deal with our feelings and associated thoughts it can eat away in our souls, even and especially if we bury them under outward displays of 'faith' and activity 'for God'.

Bill Johnson has given very wise advice for dealing with such situations based on his own experience of his father dying of cancer. This was even whilst he was declaring his church, Bethel, Redding, California, was a 'cancer-free zone'. They saw many people healed of cancer. But his own father died. He spoke very movingly on the Sunday after his father died about the unique 'sacrifice of praise' we can bring in such situations. Our praise and worship are 'flavoured' with a grief and mourning which we won't know in heaven.

The following process and acrostic is based on an adaptation of his teaching.[35] It is a way of working out and applying

---

35 See Randy Clarke and Bill Johnson, *Essential Guide to Healing*, pp and for example, https://www.youtube.com/watch?v=gLCLdFR371w

'above all else, guard your heart, for it is the wellspring of life'. It is aimed at helping us keep 'soft hearts' at all times towards the Lord and other people. Hearts to receive and be loved. To listen and love, and to keep being available for the Lord to use us to help heal others even as He heals us.

SOFT HEARTS

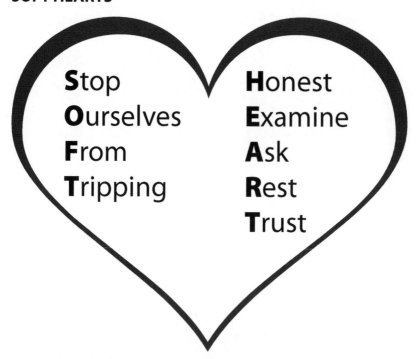

Stop **H**onest
Ourselves **E**xamine
From **A**sk
Tripping **R**est
Trust

The key five steps are:

- **Honest**: we must be completely honest and open with God. We acknowledge our pain, grief, and bewilderment. For me this was most acute in the days and years after my brother-in-law committed suicide. But in our honesty, we don't accuse God.

Cast all your anxiety on him because he cares for you. (1 Peter 5:7)

- **Examine**: my heart is open before Him as, with His help, I ask Him to 'search me' and 'know my heart'. What is behind my reactions and feelings? What is it saying about my beliefs?

Search me, God, and know my heart; test me and know my anxious thoughts. See if there is any offensive way in me, and lead me in the way everlasting. (Psalm 139:23-24)

- **Ask**: I ask Him to reveal and speak to me. I burrow into His word, especially the Psalms. Walter Brueggemann[36] describes the psalms reflecting our three experiences of 'orientation, disorientation, and reorientation'. In times of deep disorientation, grief, and confusion we can find our turmoil reflected here in the words and experiences of the psalmists. They give language to our pain and aching. The Psalms of lament can give words to express our grief. The sense of being able to echo ancient pain helps us feel heard and held by the Lord. And helps us into 'reorientation'. In hindsight I recall at university, in much less difficult circumstances, that whenever I was

---

36 Walter Brueggemann, *Spirituality of the Psalms* (Minneapolis, MN: Fortress Press, 2002).

'down' I learnt that a mix of grapefruit segments, the music of U2 and my Bible – especially the Psalms – always changed how I felt!

How long, O LORD? Will you forget me forever? How long will you hide your face from me? How long must I take counsel in my soul and have sorrow in my heart all the day? (Psalm 13:1-2 ESV)

The singer-songwriter Martyn Joseph expressed this experience well in a song; even if there are no answers, we can 'treasure the questions'.[37]

> *Treasure the questions as they rage in my mind*
> *I treasure the questions some day I will find*
> *You see I ran out of answers such a long time ago*
> *And I treasure the questions wherever I go*

- **Rest**: we seek and wait until His peace comes. His arms embrace us, and His peace surrounds us. I still might not understand but I have let Him have my heart again. I'm 're-orientated'. I'll never forget meeting 'Ann' in an outreach in Budapest. She asked for more of God's love. As her Hungarian friend and I prayed it became clear she had 'father issues'. I found another member of the team, an experienced Christian woman, who ministered to the issues from childhood sexual abuse. As she

---

37 *Treasure the Questions* written by Martyn Jospeh copyright © 1988

Broken heart, by Sam Horne

forgave her father and released him, she was restored and freed. She received beautiful affirmation and love from the Father Himself. She spoke of how she could see and feel herself on Father God's lap. She said she never wanted to leave that place!

There is no fear in love. But perfect love drives out fear, because fear has to do with punishment. The one who fears is not made perfect in love. (1 John 4:18)

- **Trust:** as we press in through the pain with our sacrifice of praise we work out our trust in Him. We develop a renewed determination to persevere. We know that victory lies ahead.

Though the fig-tree does not bud and there are no grapes on the vines, though the olive crop fails and the fields produce no food, though there are no sheep in the sheepfold and no cattle in the stalls, yet I will rejoice in the LORD, I will be joyful in God my Saviour. (Habukkuk 3:17-18)

I recently attended the funeral of an amazing young man, Rory, who died after a brave, courageous, full and faith-filled thirty-two years. We had prayed together many times. He was always so encouraging with a wisdom beyond his years and a depth of faith beyond the ordinary. Someone reported Rory had commented on Philippians 4:6-7:

Do not be anxious about anything, but in every situation, by prayer and petition, with thanksgiving, present your requests to God. And the peace of God, which transcends all understanding, will guard your hearts and your minds in Christ Jesus.

He said that in order to experience the "peace beyond understanding", we might need to give up our right to understanding.

THE CHALLENGE OF LEADING THROUGH PAIN

As leaders it is particularly important that we keep soft hearts. The spiritual attacks and just day-to-day onslaught of Christian leadership can easily mean we are hurt or even take offence at fellow believers or other leaders. We need to guard our hearts and teach our members how to do so.

Therefore, since we are surrounded by such a great cloud of witnesses, let us throw off everything that hinders and the sin that so easily entangles. And let us run with perseverance the race marked out for us, fixing our eyes on Jesus, the pioneer and perfecter of faith. For the joy set before him he endured the cross, scorning its shame, and sat down at the right hand of the throne of God. Consider him who endured such opposition from sinners, so that you will not grow weary and lose heart. (Hebrews 12:1-3)

Our honest and vulnerable accounts of our own struggles and experience can help others to make sense of their lived experience. To know they are not alone in disappointment, fear, and grief. But also to know they don't need to stay there or to fear

Overcoming Fear: Dealing with Disappointment

stepping out once again. We need to be empathetic and gentle, and full of faith and courage. In John 11 we read that Jesus comforted Martha and Mary, and wept for His friend Lazarus. And then He raised him to life again!

We need to persevere and press on. As the Canadian songwriter Bruce Cockburn[38] put it:

> *But nothing worth having comes without some kind of fight*
> *Got to kick at the darkness 'til it bleeds daylight*

Let us be those leaders who don't need to pretend we've got it all together but let us hold on to Him who has gone before. Let's walk with Jesus in radical, courageous faith – not afraid to weep with those who weep, nor rejoice with those who rejoice.

---

38 *Lovers in a Dangerous Time* written by Bruce Cockburn. Warner/Chappell Music, Inc.

6

A SIMPLE MODEL FOR PRAYING FOR THE SICK: HEAL

"Jesus did not command us to pray for the sick. He commanded us to heal them."

Bill Johnson

HOW TO PRAY FOR THE SICK

One of the key needs of many Christians and churches is to know how to pray for the sick – or, more accurately, how to heal people in Jesus' name! This is the challenge of getting going as a church, described as stage 2 in chapter 2

Jesus told His first disciples to teach others to do as He did in the Great Commission.

Then Jesus came to them and said, 'All authority in heaven and on earth has been given to me. Therefore, go and make disciples of all nations, baptising them in the name of the Father and of the Son and of the Holy Spirit, and teaching them to obey everything I have commanded you. And surely I am with you always, to the very end of the age.' (Mathew 28:18-20)

A Simple Model for Praying for the Sick: HEAL

The following simple mnemonic is offered to help people learn and remember how to pray for healing.[39] It is modelled on how Jesus and His followers prayed:

Hear from the person and the Holy Spirit
Exercise faith by praying (command/ask)
Ask what's happening
Love, affirm, and encourage

The first step is **Hear** what the person reports is their problem. We don't have to wait for people to ask for prayer. If we see someone in need we can ask them, especially if we sense the Holy Spirit leading us. But for many our first lessons will be in the church setting ('the training place for the marketplace'). We need to hear from the person: what their problem is, for how long they have had it and maybe what was going on when the problem started, and from the Holy Spirit.

We then **Exercise** faith by praying as we are led. Almost always Jesus' followers prayed by commanding healing with a phrase like 'be healed in Jesus' name'. Sometimes we may be led to ask the Spirit to work and to heal. However, as explained in chapter 1, Jesus has commissioned us to pray for healing. He has given us power and authority to pray. So, we can have liberty to command sickness and pain to leave. We are speaking to the person's body and condition.

He gave them power and authority to drive out all demons and to cure diseases, and he sent them out to proclaim the kingdom

---

39 This is based on, and consistent with, the five-step prayer model taught by John Wimber, Global Awakening and others. It is a deliberate simplification and seeks to encourage believers to focus on the key essentials of healing prayer.

of God and to heal the sick. (Luke 9:1b-2)

Critically we then **Ask** what's happening. This was something I always used to be hesitant to do – in case nothing was happening. As if it depends on me rather than our faithful and loving God! We might find out that the pain has started to reduce, or they have started to feel something, typically warmth or tingling. We can then pray again and repeat the process until the pain has gone or the condition has cleared up. Sometimes the person tells us the pain has moved which indicates a spirit of affliction (see later). We typically stop praying if the person asks us to, or after a number of attempts if nothing seems to have happened.

Don't be worried about also asking someone else to pray too. I was praying for someone with pain in their foot recently at church – the pain level went down by fifty per cent but seemed stuck. I asked a child I knew nearby if they would pray? I asked them just to ask Jesus to heal the foot – they prayed and all the pain went! Children are great healers as they have not learnt to not expect healing! People who have just been healed of a certain problem are also great to get to pray for similar problems as their faith levels are definitely up!

Finally, **Love.** I remember when I had the transformative privilege of going on an 'International Mission Trip' with Dr Randy Clarke to Brazil in 2014. He impressed on us, his ministry team of circa fifty people, that whatever happened to the people we prayed for, they must always experience love and compassion from us. We cannot choose or guarantee healing – it's God's power at work through us but we can always choose to love people and treat them with dignity and respect.

If we have not seen any apparent healing, encourage the person by saying something always happens when we pray. Often, we can see healing come later. Assure them of our love and the Lord's, and encourage them to keep seeking healing prayer.

If they have reported full or partial healing then encourage them to give thanks for their healing, share their testimony and critically sustain their healing.

A SCRIPT FOR HEALING

Somewhat to my and others' surprise in The Turning we have found that a simple script for sharing the gospel can be incredibly effective. So, in similar vein, I offer a simple 'script' for praying for healing below. This is especially intended for use outside the church with non-believers and can be naturally linked into evangelism using The Turning script or similar.

It is inspired by teaching from Julian Richards, leader of New Wine Wales, and a link to a message by him is found in Appendix/Resources section at the end of this book. It is intended to give confidence and a helpful starting point rather than be prescriptive or limiting.

The words used obviously need to be adapted for the context and circumstances. The following 'script' assumes you see or hear someone in obvious need of healing and/or are prompted by the Holy Spirit. We need to learn to hear the Father and only do what He is doing. In learning to do this we will sometimes get it wrong, but we'll only learn by stepping out. As long as our motive and approach are love then we can only bless people.

A Simple Model for Praying for the Sick: HEAL

Script	Notes/guidance
Hello my name is <insert your name>. You seem to have a problem with <insert their issue>.	They will often tell you more. Briefly ask them what the problem is, how long they have had it, and what the doctors say.
This may sound weird but in my church, we pray for people with problems like yours and they often get better. Would you like me to pray for you now?	If they say no thank you, just accept graciously and bless them. If they say you can pray for me later or at home, suggest that you're just learning and praying from a distance is like PhD prayer. You find it works much better hands on and you'll be really quick.
Please repeat after me, 'Lord Jesus, please heal me.'	Wait for them to say this.
Please come, Holy Spirit. Pain go! I command <their problem> be gone/healed in Jesus' name.	Keep it short and simple as informed by what they have told you.
How's the problem/pain now? Please test it out?	See what's happened. If they are not totally healed pray again briefly – you can do this a few times if they are willing. But stop as soon as they have had enough!
That's great – Jesus has healed you/started healing you! We thank Him!	They may have questions about what's happened. As prompted you can share more about Jesus and/or arrange to meet them/direct them to a church/suggest they read a gospel at home. They will find Jesus healed people all the time!
(If no apparent healing): I am sorry you've not been healed yet. I don't know why but I will keep praying. May God bless you!	You can say that we see people healed half the time (or whatever your experience is) – we don't know why but you are happy to keep praying, or will pray for them again. Be friendly, encouraging, and bless them.

A Simple Model for Praying for the Sick: HEAL

My friend Michael recently took part in The Turning Mission to Scotland. This is his testimony of praying simply for healing:

> *I was on the streets of Glasgow with a lovely lady from Ghana. She approached this elderly lady and started going through the script[40] with her. She said she was Catholic and Edna explained that it was important that we invited Jesus into our lives; the lady said that she would if she had to. At this point I intervened as I did not want her to say the prayer because I did not want her to be coerced into saying the prayer. I gave her a copy of the script and said she could pray it later.*
>
> *She had a walking stick and I asked her if she suffered from arthritis? (This was not a word of knowledge.[41]) She said no and went on to explain that she had broken her hip; it had been surgically repaired but had not healed properly. She said that it felt that a bolt had come loose.*
>
> *I asked if she was in pain and she said yes. I asked if I could pray, explaining some of my history, and she permitted me to do so. After getting permission I placed my hand on her arm and in the name of Jesus I commanded the pain to go and the hip to be healed. I questioned her if there was any improvement and she said yes. I asked if I could pray again and she said yes. Before I started I asked her what the pain level was, she said it was an eight and now it was a four. After praying again it went down to zero!*

---

40 The Turning script, which gives an opportunity for people to hear that God loves them, is a basic outline of the gospel and an opportunity to invite Jesus into their lives.

41 Michael has seen lots of people healed with arthritis!

A Simple Model for Praying for the Sick: HEAL

THERE'S NO ONE WAY

God heals in so many ways (see below), that the last thing I am suggesting is that the above is *the* way to pray for healing. It is *a* way and intended to help people start. But be prepared to see the Lord surprise and amaze you in how He heals.

Francis MacNutt in his seminal book *Healing*,[42] relates a wonderful story relating to the often-quoted requirement for faith to be present at least in the prayer minister. A cessationist ministerial friend of his was preaching and wanted to illustrate to a group of college students that their faith could depend on God's revealed truth and they didn't need 'gimmicks' like healing for their faith. So, at the start of his talk, he called out anyone who needed healing and sought to imitate the healing evangelists he derided by placing his hands forcibly on people and saying 'be healed' loudly. He asked everyone how they were, ready to make his point, when, to his chagrin, they all said they were healed! At least three quarters were still healed the next day.

I am continually reminded that God has a sense of humour and will defy any and every attempt we might make to put Him in a box. We can never prescribe a method or rely on an expectation that God will always do what we expect. But we can rely on His nature as faithful, good, and loving, and so see Him heal people as it expresses who He is.

THE LORD HEALS IN MANY WAYS

God is a healer. It's in His nature, as Exodus reminds us. Whilst

---

42 Francis MacNutt, *Healing* (Hodder & Stoughton, 1989).

A Simple Model for Praying for the Sick: HEAL

I have outlined a recommended approach to healing through one-to-one prayer, I am continually reminded that God can and does heal in many ways.

Firstly, it is important to realise that our bodies have been created to heal though natural processes. Medical science intervenes by aligning with and supporting these. Here's my initial but growing list of how God heals, with an illustration and biblical references. I pray you would see God heal in even more ways!

- **Natural processes**: our bodies are 'fearfully and wonderfully made' to fight infection, recover from sickness, and heal wounds. (Psalm 139:14)
- **Medicine**: clinicians can use their scientific understanding of sickness, disease, and injury to diagnose what's wrong with us, and use advice and treatments to aid or supplement natural recovery processes. (1 Timothy 5:23, Mark 2:27)
- **Intercessory prayer**: when we pray for people at a distance. Almost all churches will do this, faithfully praying for God's comfort and healing for people. Although I call this 'PhD prayer' there are published research studies[43] showing it works as well as one's questioning the effect. Pete Greig recounts the compelling story of Floyd McClung's daughter and new grandson 'triple miracle'.[44] (James 5:15)

---

43 http://www.is-there-a-god.info/life/ipstudies/

44 Pete Greig, *God on Mute* (David C. Cook, 2007) pp 106-114.

A Simple Model for Praying for the Sick: HEAL

- **Anointing with oil**: this is a commonly practised and deeply biblical method in many churches. It is often used for people with chronic illness and in deliverance. (James 5:14)
- **Platform prayer**: on a number of occasions recently, as I have stood up to preach, I have felt prompted to share words of knowledge (prompts by the Holy Spirit He wants to heal people – but wait for the next chapter for more!). In my own church, I asked any people with these problems – shoulder pain, back pain, and foot pain – to stand up. I asked those around them to stretch out their hands towards them and I prayed for their healing. About ten people stood – over half reported partial or full healing. The rest were encouraged to come for prayer after the service. Preaching recently in India I did the same, with maybe twenty-five people reporting healing! Randy Clark (and others) see hundreds healed like this! (James 5:15)
- **Laying on of hands**: this is part of the basic HEAL approach described above, modelled on Jesus' practice. Earlier this week at an interview, one of the other candidates obviously had a problem with his wrist. I asked what was up: he'd had sharp pain there since the morning; I asked if I could pray. I laid hands on him and immediately all his pain went! (Matthew 8:14-15, Luke 4:40)
- **Prayer for healing**: this is part of the basic HEAL approach described above. I have received prayer myself

A Simple Model for Praying for the Sick: HEAL

for knee pain that had threatened to stop me running a half marathon. I was healed through healing prayer, and ran the full thirteen-and-half miles the next week! (Acts 3:2-6)

- **Prayer for self**: I encourage people to pray for themselves and often find it effective as I fight through the various aches and pains that can assault me when I'm out running! (Isaiah 40:31)

- **Proclaiming Jesus**: this one may shift you out of your comfort zone – it did me. I was at a conference in Nigeria and one of the speakers, 'Apostle Mike', spoke one evening. All he preached on for forty-five minutes was how amazing and powerful the name of Jesus was. He then asked anyone who needed healing to come to the front, and fifty people came up. He proclaimed the name of Jesus over them and forty were healed straight away. Somewhat out of my comfort zone, I was asked to join him in praying for the remaining ten – we laid hands on and proclaimed Jesus over them, and they were all either instantaneously healed or fell over under the Holy Spirit's anointing. The 'only' prayer uttered was 'Jesus'! Truly there is power in the name of Jesus! (Acts 3:4-8)

- **Word of God**: just receiving the truth of God as expressed in His word can lead to healing. There is power in the word! (Proverbs 4:20-23)

- **Declaration**: sometimes people need to speak and declare their own alignment with Jesus and His truth in order to receive healing as David testified in the Psalms. This is a particular emphasis of the 'word of faith' movement. (Psalm 30:2 and 118:17, Mark 11:24)

- **Acts of obedience**: often there is a point when praying for people, when we ask them to 'do something they could not do before'. This requires them to exercise faith and maybe take a risk such as get out of a wheelchair, walk without a crutch, or try a movement that caused pain before. To see the shock on people's faces when they can walk without pain or raise a frozen shoulder is priceless! There are many testimonies showing this at **https://globalawakening.com/ testimonies**. (Acts 3:7-8, Luke 17:11-14)

- **Repentance and confession**: refusal to repent of sin can have serious consequences as Jesus taught us – spiritually, emotionally, and physically. By no means all sickness is caused by sin, but it can be. So we need to be aware of this and ready to prompt people as the Spirit leads. God is always ready to embrace us in our mess when we come to Him in humility. (James 5:16, 1 John 1:9)

- **Special places**: there are many places that Christians over many years have associated with healing, such as Lourdes and nowadays certain cities in South America. Whether we think it's the expectancy and faith stirred up in pilgrims and visitors, Holy Spirit revival power, centuries of prayer, 'thin places' where heaven is close, angelic activity, or anointing on the land (or some combination/we don't know), God seems to love to do

A Simple Model for Praying for the Sick: HEAL

things beyond our expectations. (John 5:1-15 Pool of Bethseda, and John 9:1-11 Pool of Siloam)

- **Counselling**: sometimes being able to understand and name issues, especially around inner wounds and trauma, can bring insight and healing. My own family's journey to recover from a family member's suicide was greatly helped by godly counselling. (John 14:26, Hebrews 4:15)

- **Art**: there is an art wall in our church and recently a visitor came in, saw the painting below[45] and burst into tears. The lady said she was hit by a wave of God's love coming off the page and fell to the ground sobbing as God ministered beautifully to her heart. The painting touched something deep within her and brought healing and restoration.

---

45 Painting by Sammy Horne. See http://www.samhorneart.co.uk/

A Simple Model for Praying for the Sick: HEAL

- **Worship**: sometimes God just breaks in during worship and heals! We know He inhabits the praises of His people (see Psalm 22:3 KJV). At a conference at Bethel Church, I recall that every time we sang a particular song, I cried. It was only later I realised the Lord had healed something deep in me during the worship. (1 Samuel 16:23, Psalm 103)
- **Music**: it is perhaps no surprise that music itself can bring deep emotional healing to people – and if emotional healing then physical healing often follows. (1 Samuel 16:14-23)
- **Dance and flagging**: our church dance and flag team have seen people healed as they have danced and many enter into new freedom. (Psalm 30:11-12)
- **Angels**: the Bible speaks of angels as ministers of God's grace and this includes healing. I believe this is often the way the Lord moves and works. (Psalms 103 and 104, Hebrews 1)
- **Words of knowledge**: the next chapter will explain and illustrate how words of knowledge work. There are many, many examples also at **https://globalawakening. com/testimonies**. (Mark 2:8)
- **Testimony**: as we release testimony and story of what Jesus has done for others in healing, the prophetic invitation is given to do that again for people. I have seen many people healed just watching videos or listening to other people's testimonies! At a healing seminar one summer at our church camp, we saw some people healed and then we got them to pray for others

A Simple Model for Praying for the Sick: HEAL

with similar conditions – a crazy and beautiful chain reaction of healing was released! (Revelation 19:10)

- **Inner/emotional healing**: at a recent meeting I was praying for one of the prayer team. She had back pain but after a couple of prayers we'd only seen limited improvement. I sensed it was linked to her carrying anxiety about her family. After encouraging her to lay this down and praying for *shalom* (peace), the back pain went completely! (Psalm 34:17-20, Romans 8:15-16)

- **Change thinking and speaking**: neuroscience backs up the ancient biblical truth that how we think and speak influences our bodies – including neural pathways, enzymes and hormone levels. Noticing how we think and asking God to bring our thoughts and speech into line with His truth is powerful and often brings both inner and physical healing. We prayed recently at our Healing Rooms with a lady who'd had negative things spoken over her as a teenager that had warped her sense of worth; as we identified these and she acknowledged them and accepted the truth about herself, she not only felt a lot better but saw physical healing in her body too! (Romans 12:1-2)

- **Forgiveness of sin**: a man asked for prayer at the end of a healing meeting in Chelmsford. His chest tendons and muscles were misshapen, and he lacked full strength. It was an old injury from having to suddenly grab on to stop himself falling on some oil in a workshop. As I listened to him, I had the impression, I believe, from the Holy Spirit

A Simple Model for Praying for the Sick: HEAL

that he needed to forgive first. I asked him if he had forgiven himself and indeed his co-worker. He had not. He prayed a simple prayer of forgiveness. I then prayed for his muscles and tendons and over the next five or ten minutes he regained much of his strength as the tendons and muscles went back into normal shape. It was amazing! (Matthew 9:1-8)

- **Deliverance**: I will address this later in more detail, but sometimes when we pray for someone's pain, it moves around. This indicates a 'spirit of affliction' (an evil or demonic spirit causing a physical problem) that we can cast out in the name of Jesus. Problems from accidents are also often associated with a 'spirit of trauma'. I prayed with a lady recently who reported neck problems from an accident many years ago – when I broke off the spirit of trauma from her, the physical pains went. (Luke 8:26-39)

- **Justice**: Isaiah 58 highlights a core teaching of the Bible: our healing is related to our pursuit of justice and integrity.

- **Generosity to the poor**: the Bible teaches our healing is also related to our generosity. A lifestyle of open-heartedness brings *shalom* (the biblical sense of complete health and well-being). (Isaiah 58:7-8)

- **Fasting**: as Jesus taught, sometimes we need as prayers to fast to bring healing but Isaiah also connects the people's true fasting, their true worship, with their healing and well-being. (Isaiah 58:6-9, Matthew 17:14-21)

A Simple Model for Praying for the Sick: HEAL

- **Serving**: Isaiah also connects people's service (an aspect of worship), with their healing and well-being. I suspect sometimes people need to learn to serve as part of resisting their mindsets and not focusing on themselves and their own needs. (Isaiah 58:7-8)

- **Cloths/handkerchiefs prayed for**: as a church once we prayed for a fellow believer in intensive care in France and anointed a tea towel. It was taken and laid on him, and he recovered. Coincidence? The craziest version of such stories is told by Cal Pierce[46] of a South African Healing Rooms team which was contacted by parents of a girl with a brain tumour so severe is was distorting her skull causing huge pain. The Holy Spirit, in the face of an apparently dodgy postal system and time demands, instructed them to pray over and anoint a cloth and then photocopy and fax the image to the parents! The parents tied a copy of the fax to her head, she broke out in sweat for three days and the tumour completely disappeared. OK I have no way of explaining that. Another marvel for the mystery box! (Acts 19:12)

- **Taking regular communion**: for example, my friend had a tear in her diaphragm that the surgeon said would not repair naturally. After a friend prayed for healing, she took communion every day for two weeks and realised the problem had disappeared! (1 Corinthians 11:27-30)

- **Points of contact**: in the Bible we see examples of

---

46 Cal Pierce, *Healing in the Kingdom: How the Power of God and Your Faith Can Heal the Sick* (Chosen Books, 2008).

bones and clothes that had come into contact with anointed people being used in healing and even resurrection. From this, traditions of 'reliquaries' have developed in some churches. Where they inspire biblical faith in Jesus you can imagine how they could be used powerfully. (Matthew 9:20-22, 2 Kings 13:20-21)

- **Blessing:** Roy Godwin from Ffald-y-Brenin Retreat Centre, tells many stories of how people are often healed when he or his team 'just' bless people in the name of the Father, Son and Holy Spirit.[47]

PRACTICAL GUIDELINES

As we learn and grow in praying for healing, it's helpful to have some practical guidelines that help safeguard everyone and establish an honouring and loving culture. These are intended as principles and guidance, not a rigid prescription. They are based on experience in my own church and exposure to other ministry protocols.

- Decide as leaders when you might want to have clearly identified (maybe with badges) people ministering and praying for healing. For example, this may be appropriate for ministry after a service or in a special healing service with many visitors. However, we are seeking to encourage and activate the *whole* church body in healing so we don't want to stop people learning and praying for

---

47 *The Way of Blessing: Stepping Into the Mission and Presence of God* by Roy Godwin. David C Cook, 2016.

A Simple Model for Praying for the Sick: HEAL

others. New Wine, for instance, invites anyone who is experienced and regularly prays for people to form their ministry teams at their annual conferences.

- Ensure that ministry team members or people praying understand they need to relate to and honour the leadership overseeing their ministry, including asking for help when they feel 'out of their depth'. Recognise your limits.

- Ensure everyone has clarity about the need for general confidentiality but that safeguarding responsibilities override this. The church's safeguarding policy and training should ensure this is understood. If ministry team members are unclear or unsure they need to raise the issue with the leader(s) overseeing their ministry. On a number of occasions people have told me that they have been abused or been the perpetrator.

- Pray ideally in pairs and for people of the same gender unless in a mixed pair.

- Introduce yourself and ensure you know their name.

- Pray out loud and in normal language.

- Laying on of hands is biblical but ask permission first, and ensure hands are placed in appropriate places such as on shoulders or back.

- Never push someone over or put pressure on them when praying.

- Pray with your eyes open. This takes practice but allows you to see what God might be doing.

- Stop praying when people have had enough but always

A Simple Model for Praying for the Sick: HEAL

encourage and affirm them.

- Don't blame people for their illness or problems, or if there is no improvement.
- Always ensure people continue to take any prescribed medication, even if they believe they are healed, until they have seen their doctor.
- Encourage people with advice as to how the keep their healing. (see page 147 on Sustaining healing)

LEARNING TO TRUST: DOING WHATEVER HE TELLS US!

God is a healer. A creative exuberant healer! I have shared a simple and proven starting approach but also many ways I have heard and seen Him heal. I encourage you to step out in faith and let the Holy Spirit lead you. As His friend John recorded in John 2, let us do what Jesus' and indeed John's own 'stepmother' Mary said when He first burst on to the Galilean scene: '*Do whatever He tells you!*'

7

GETTING GOING WITH HEALING: WORDS OF KNOWLEDGE

"Don't limit God to fit in the way that you think that He is going to speak, because just about the time that we think we have Him figured out, He will oftentimes speak to us in another way. God wants us to be in tune with Him, and not just in tune with one of the ways that He gives those words."

Randy Clark

GROWING IN FAITH TOGETHER

In helping churches and their members get started in healing (stage 2 in chapter 2), words of knowledge are a great help and can 'jump start' individuals and congregations. We can hear about healing and mentally assent to Biblical teaching, but we move to a different level of understanding and faith when we see and experience healing in ourselves and those around us.

1 Corinthians 12:4ff describes the spiritual gifts available to all believers.

There are different kinds of gifts, but the same Spirit distributes
them. There are different kinds of service, but the same Lord.
There are different kinds of working, but in all of them and
in everyone it is the same God at work. Now to each one the
manifestation of the Spirit is given for the common good. To one
there is given through the Spirit a message of wisdom, to another
a message of knowledge by means of the same Spirit, to another
faith by the same Spirit, to another gifts of healing by that one
Spirit, to another miraculous powers, to another prophecy, to
another distinguishing between spirits, to another speaking in
different kinds of tongues and to still another the interpretation
of tongues. All these are the work of one and the same Spirit, and
he distributes them to each one, just as he determines.

Last year I was journaling and asked the Lord about words of
knowledge. I felt Him say: 'Words of knowledge resonate as
they show your reliance on Me and what I the Father want to
do. They help teach you how to do what the Father does and
not your own thing.'

I recall being at a meeting for Christians as part of the team
with our minister – it was a 'tough gig' as he said. The room's
layout, the acoustics, and people's hearts seemed to make things
difficult. Our minister talked on 'Encountering Father's Presence'
and asked me to lead them into healing. I had felt the Lord
give me a word of knowledge around pain in the left arm and
wrist. I shared this, and one man responded. He had fibromyalgia,
stiffness in the arm, hypersensitivity, and tinnitus. As I prayed
he felt looser and tingling in his head. His tinnitus improved.

Getting Going with Healing: Words of Knowledge

He was then lying 'out in the Holy Spirit' on the (hard) floor for about twenty minutes. He told me afterwards that he had not been able to lie in the Spirit for many years because of his hypersensitivity. He also said his symptoms were improved. The word opened up healing and filling prayer for someone who otherwise I would never have identified but this was what the Father wanted to do.

WHAT IS A WORD OF KNOWLEDGE?

A word of knowledge is a supernatural revelation of information by the Holy Spirit. One of the reasons the Holy Spirit gives them is to prepare the way, signal His desire, create the power, and encourage faith in the hearers for healing.

In the Greek they are *rhema* words of God which indicate His 'now', in the moment intention and power to heal specific conditions, illnesses, or diseases. They contain within them the power and ability to bring the healing or miracle required, in the speaking of the words or doing of the action. This is another example of the power of God's word(s).

> *What we have received is not the spirit of the world, but the Spirit who is from God, so that we may understand what God has freely given us. This is what we speak, not in words taught us by human wisdom but in words taught by the Spirit, explaining spiritual realities with Spirit-taught words. (1 Corinthians 2:12-13)*

We see Jesus using words of knowledge in Mark 2 where He knew what people were thinking about the paralytic man, and in

John 4 where He knew the Samaritan woman had many husbands.

*A few days later, when Jesus again entered Capernaum, the people heard that he had come home. They gathered in such large numbers that there was no room left, not even outside the door, and he preached the word to them. Some men came, bringing to him a paralysed man, carried by four of them. Since they could not get him to Jesus because of the crowd, they made an opening in the roof above Jesus by digging through it and then lowered the mat the man was lying on. When Jesus saw their faith, he said to the paralysed man, 'Son, your sins are forgiven.' Now some teachers of the law were sitting there, thinking to themselves, 'Why does this fellow talk like that? He's blaspheming! Who can forgive sins but God alone?' **Immediately Jesus knew in his spirit** that this was what they were thinking in their hearts, and he said to them, 'Why are you thinking these things? Which is easier: to say to this paralysed man, "Your sins are forgiven," or to say, "Get up, take your mat and walk"? But I want you to know that the Son of Man has authority on earth to forgive sins.' So, he said to the man, 'I tell you, get up, take your mat, and go home.' He got up, took his mat and walked out in full view of them all. This amazed everyone, and they praised God, saying, 'We have never seen anything like this!' (Mark 2:1-12)*

Prophetic revelation and words of knowledge are two sides of a coin. Often prophetic gifted people don't realise this, so it can be very releasing.

Different church congregations will have a different general understanding and expectation about how words of knowledge work. The more people understand that a word of knowledge is an invitation to be healed, the more they are likely to respond with faith. Thus, in South America over half the people responding to a word of knowledge can be healed just hearing the word. The same applies to hearing about or seeing a similar miracle to the one they need.

HOW DO YOU RECEIVE A WORD OF KNOWLEDGE?

There are classically seven different ways in which words of knowledge can be given by the Holy Spirit (as I have read and heard taught by Dr Randy Clarke and Blaine Cook). They are typically different ways our bodies, minds, and spirits interact with the Holy Spirit to receive some revelation of what He wants to do. Sometimes these can come in a church service, when we specifically ask for them, as we pray for someone's healing to guide us or, of course, in our normal everyday lives. I have added a couple more ways I have heard or seen.

- **Pain or sensation in part of body**: we perceive pains, sensations, or feelings, which are not ours normally.

For example, one Sunday morning at church, I felt a twinge of pain in my left shoulder. I perceived this to be a word of knowledge and gave it at the end of the service. Three people came for prayer, all who reported their pain leaving. Then Richard came, who reported that he had had his shoulder joint replaced over twenty-five years ago and had pain as well as twenty-five years of restricted movement. When we prayed using a simple command prayer all the pain went and, to his amazement, he found he had regained near normal movement of his arm and shoulder. Somewhat amusingly and as a reminder of the need for careful post-prayer advice, he was so taken with his healed shoulder he went and rebuilt a shed – and overdid it, using muscles for the first time in many years. Somewhat sheepishly he came for prayer again the next week – and again all the pain left on command. Over the past year he has told me on a number of occasions how his shoulder is getting stronger – he has a ready measure as he does archery! What used to be full draw weight for him now feels limp!

Sometimes we can feel the word of knowledge is a little strange and we can be uncomfortable giving it, but I've learnt to trust God. Recently at a conference in Southampton, I felt and gave a word of knowledge of nipple pain. A lady bounded up and told me she had had a mastectomy and only that morning had been talking with her husband about the nipple pain she had. I commanded all pain to go and it did. She was blessed to know that God cared about what she had regarded as a 'small thing'.

This category can also include emotions that you feel which aren't yours normally!

- **Impression**: for an example see Jesus in Mark 2 with the paralytic man. This can just come to our minds – we literally think the word.

Dave came to me to ask for prayer at the end of a healing meeting in Chelmsford. His chest tendons and muscles were misshapen, and he lacked full strength. It was an old injury from having to suddenly grab on to stop himself falling on some oil in a workshop. As I listened to him, I had the impression from the Holy Spirit that he needed to forgive first. I asked him if he had forgiven himself and indeed his co-worker. He had not. He prayed a simple prayer of forgiveness. I then prayed for his muscles and tendons and over the next five or ten minutes he regained much of his strength as the tendons and muscles went back into normal shape.

- **Picture of word**: for these words of knowledge people can see a word. A prophetic friend sees the word above people's heads.
- **Fleeting or short vision**: we just see a picture of something happening or perhaps see a body part. It's important to say what you see and not interpret it.

A Californian friend recently was prophesying over me on a mission trip. She told me to go with the wave of God that was coming. Later I told her the picture the Lord had given me earlier in the year of riding on a surfboard, sitting on a chair. Jesus was the surfer! My friend indeed saw me on the surfboard and wasn't sure that as a Brit I'd get the surfing bit!

- **Open vision**: some people have full-blown open visions which can be words of knowledge.

- **Smell**: some people have reported smelling something unusual which points to something the Lord wants to do.
- **Speaking**: sometimes we find ourselves just saying something in an unpremeditated way! This can happen especially when we are praying for people and it can unlock situations.
- **Dream**: we have memorable dreams that we sense might be from the Lord.

I recently had a dream that, unusually for me, I remembered on waking. It featured our minister's wife's back being healed by something clearly coming into alignment and then a cut away to me with a work colleague. I pondered this and was asking the Lord what it meant. I had not considered the most obvious meaning! Then I happened to sit behind her the following Sunday in church and saw her grab her back. I asked her and found she had been in agony for a month with a bad back. After prayer the pain went and later in the week she reported the back was still much better.

An interesting other recent example was from my friend Ian when we were at a Randy Clarke conference. In a dream he saw Dr Randy give out a word of knowledge. Ian gave the word of knowledge he heard Randy say – a rare woman's name, Martini, and medical condition. A lady called Martini indeed responded and was healed!

- **Hearing**: Some people can also hear the condition, issue, or a name.

LEARNING TO WALK IN WORDS OF KNOWLEDGE

I am not sure if these are even exhaustive given the creativity of the Holy Spirit! I mainly receive words of knowledge through pains or sensations in my body and sometimes impressions or the occasional dreams. I have challenged myself over the last year to identify and give words of knowledge that may feel weaker and to press into new ways of receiving. This involves more risk but can have more impact.

I would encourage everyone to ask for the gift of words of knowledge and to seek impartation. We ask, expect, and practise. Go for it. In any church setting as leaders, we should be ready to explain words of knowledge: what they are, how we receive them and critically give people a chance to practise. Every time there is such teaching, I find many people who have never received words of knowledge, receive one and are so encouraged when people respond and are healed.

In bringing words of knowledge we must be neither arrogant nor falsely humble. In bringing words of knowledge in a meeting we should submit to the leadership and authority of those leading the meeting. It is OK to say we are nervous or not sure. As John Wimber said, 'Faith is spelt R-I-S-K.' However, what's the worst that can happen? No one responds, and we look silly. Or that we stay quiet and someone misses their miracle? I would urge you to particularly be brave in the most faint and fleeting words of knowledge – feelings, visions, words, etc.

I would also encourage leaders to teach their churches to help people who are learning about words of knowledge by responding! In Brazil and other contexts where people really understand words of knowledge, people jump up when they hear the word and half of them are healed even before prayer. The word contains the power itself.

LED BY THE LORD

Sometimes the Lord gives us words to lead us into what He wants to do. In February 2017 I had the opportunity to join a good friend, Jo Moody, and her team from Agape Freedom Fighters, at a conference on life with the Lord and healing at a church in St Alban's about fifty miles from home. Jo and her team from the US were in the UK for about two weeks though I was only able to be with them for a day. I had joined them the previous year for a healing service at the same church as part of her ministry team.

The focus of the day was essentially on our adoption as children of God. In the afternoon, I was walking round seeing if anyone wanted prayer and kept being drawn to a woman who was already receiving ministry from one of the team. The team member beckoned me over and asked me to join her. As she said later, she'd been praying for some time and felt she needed some more 'firepower'. It turned out she had taken the lady, 'Diane', on an amazing journey of inner healing. She had presented as physically very tense, stressed, and with constant neck and shoulder pain. They had been through a process of releasing forgiveness and as she had done this, and we now prayed for her physically, the stress and pain were leaving. We were using prayers of command for pain to go and petition to ask the Lord to release His Spirit of peace and joy and to restore her. Her scrunched up neck appeared to grow by about an inch. She was visibly taller and brighter! And was so happy.

As we finished and moved to post-prayer advice we asked if she planned to come to the evening healing service. She explained that she was and how she was bringing her sister and her family who had such great needs. As she started to explain, I asked their names and realised I had prayed for some of them the previous year! Her sister, 'Ann', had lost so much hope – she had a child with some behavioural and neurological issues, including OCD, and an estranged partner.

She told me she had wanted to find me to tell me what had happened! It suddenly felt like the Lord has set this up. My draw to her in hindsight was probably a form of word of knowledge.

I recall meeting the mum and her child the year before and hearing how tough things were. As they described things it sounded like spiritual attack as well as bad OCD. I had interviewed the mum and child as much as I could, as they were both very anxious. I recall just praying petition prayers asking for shalom and the Holy Spirit to fill them. The child 'rested' beautifully in the Spirit through much of the evening.

Anyway, Diane told me after the healing service the previous year that the child had been, in her words, healed of the OCD.

They now wanted more prayer given the ongoing challenges. I was encouraged they were returning but alas, I could not stay for the healing service so trusted the rest of the team to pick up the family (it's always about Jesus and team!). We did pray that the whole family would encounter the Lord and His healing power.

WORDS OF KNOWLEDGE

I would encourage you and, through you, all your church members, to ask for the gift of words of knowledge and to seek impartation. Ask, expect, and practise. We need to teach and explain words of knowledge: what they are, how we receive them and critically give people a chance to practise. Every such time, I find many people who have never received words of knowledge, are activated! I recently taught our youth group on this topic – and they were straight into receiving words and seeing healing! Many said it was their favourite session of the year. Whether children, youth, or mature adults, whether new or seasoned Christians, God wants to use us all to demonstrate His goodness and love.

Carrying the glory, by Jenny Whitfield

8

GROWING TOGETHER: HEALING AND WHOLENESS

"One of the most clarifying definitions of ministry then, is doing the kind of things that Jesus did for the same reason that He did them."

Alan Hirsch

GROWING IN UNDERSTANDING

How we think of and understand the world, our worldview, governs how we behave and our expectations. This is a key area in healing for people and churches wanting to press into greater understanding and experience, in the stages 3 and 4 described in chapter 2.

One of the powerful things I have learnt especially from Peter Horrobin and Dr Randy Clark is the importance of good solid and biblical teaching. This creates a foundation for and understanding of how God works in healing. Indeed, Dr Randy's PhD explores six things that increase the likelihood of healing related to metal-related[48] miracles and healings. One of these is a biblical and practical experience and understanding of healing.

How we think is critical to how we experience and perceive the world. If people believe that healing is not for today or is at best rare then they will not expect to get healed. That's why non-Christians who have no negative expectations can be easier to pray for!

I recall putting into practice Julian Richard's teaching[49] about praying for non-Christians in the supermarket one Sunday as I went to get a last-minute family lunch. The shop assistant at the delicatessen counter was crouched over by the hot rotisserie chickens. As I asked for a chicken she went to get up, very slowly and gingerly. I said, 'You look in pain,' and she told me she had bad sciatic nerve and back pain. I said, 'This may sound strange but in my church, we pray for people with pain like yours and they often get healed. Would you like me to pray for you?'

She said yes please. So as soon as she had wrapped up my hot chicken, I said, 'Please say, "Lord Jesus, please heal me."' She did. I then asked the Holy Spirit to come and commanded the pain to go and the hip to be healed. I asked if there was a change and she said it was somewhat better. I prayed again. This time all the pain had gone. She was flabbergasted. I told her it was Jesus and to thank Him and tell the pain to go in

---

48 'Metal-related miracles' are where someone has metal or some other foreign substance implanted in their body as part of a medical procedure. This might include prostheses, artificial joints, screws and plates, etc. Obviously the 'dissolving' or movement of these is demonstrable by X-ray, hence the opportunity to gather compelling evidence!

49 See Appendix/Resources section for the link.

Growing Together: Healing and Wholeness

His name if it came back.

I went off to find my son, who had sharply disappeared up the next aisle as soon as he had realised what was about to happen! I saw the assistant excitedly telling her colleague what had happened, and they were laughing! She had no 'grid' or framework to not expect to be healed! The kingdom of God was manifested to her.

HEALING AND WHOLENESS

So, we need to grow in understanding. One of the areas to grow together is the linkage between physical, emotional, spiritual, and relational health. Peter Horrobin writes that 'healing is the restoration of God's order to the spirit, soul and body'. Jesus ministered to all these aspects of people to bring them wholeness through physical and inner/emotional healing and deliverance. We must do the same. Medical science has increasingly come to understand the connection between mental and psychological health and physical health. It is now estimated that eighty-five per cent of physical problems have some contributory emotional root.[50]

The diagram[51] below illustrates how the current scientific understanding of system biology has helped us to appreciate much better the complex interplay of genetics, lifestyle, and environment on our health. Systems biology extends our understanding of the determinants of health downwards in

---

50 Craig Miller and Dr Randy Clark have written really helpfully on this in *Finding Victory When Healing Doesn't Happen* (Global Awakening, 2015). This includes a useful appendix of common linkages between emotional issues and physical conditions.

51 Diagram from *Health Beyond the Fog: a future for public healthcare*, prepared for the Royal Free Charity, 2018.

scale from organs to genes; and upwards to encompass behavioural, social, and environmental levels. The interactions of these determine how the predispositions of genes express themselves into the physical manifestation of the phenotype (that is the observable characteristics which are expressing the underlying genetic inheritance).

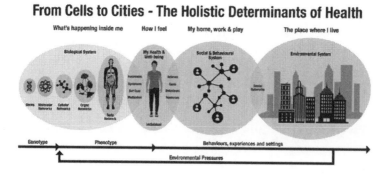

From Cells to Cities - The Holistic Determinants of Health

This is no surprise as we are whole people. The Hebraic mindset would always see people as one and *shalom* as encompassing a holistic peace and health. Science today can increasingly map the links between our brain function, thought patterns, endocrine and nervous systems, and physical health.

We are integrated beings: body, soul, and spirit.

- **Body:** our organs, musculo-skeletal system, reproductive system, digestive and elimination systems, cardiovascular system, brain, and senses, and the underlying and linked biochemical, neural, immune, and endocrine (hormonal) systems.
- **Soul:** typically described as being made up of three

Growing Together: Healing and Wholeness

parts of our minds (conscious and unconscious thinking), emotions (feelings), and will (choices).

- **Spirit:** the source of meaning and purpose, where we can enter into life and fellowship with God.

Paul wrote of our three-part integrated nature in his letter to the Thessalonian church.

May God himself, the God of peace, sanctify you through and through. May your whole spirit, soul and body be kept blameless at the coming of our Lord Jesus Christ. (1 Thessalonians 5:23)

We are complex beings, wonderfully made, as Psalm 139 reminds us, and we live within families, communities, and environment, and many of us study or work in schools, colleges, and workplaces. All of these can be health promoting and life enhancing – or they can drain life, and cause illness and harm. The diagram on the next page illustrates this.

It's no surprise therefore that issues, wounds, or attacks which arise in any area of us as people or indeed our wider environment as above can affect us in our bodies, souls and/or spirits. The Apostle John taught that our physical and spiritual health are related:

Beloved, I pray that you may prosper in all things and be in health, just as your soul prospers. (3 John 1:2 NKJV)

So as we learn to minister to people, we need to develop a

greater awareness of the possible root causes of presenting issues, and indeed how immediate and crucially sustained healing may come. We can gain an insight into some of these issues as we ask people simple questions and critically we listen to the Holy Spirit.

EMOTIONAL AND INNER HEALING

I met Louise in Southampton when I was privileged to be on the ministry team at a Global Awakening Conference with Randy Clark. She came with severe pain (10/10) in her shoulders. I followed the prayer model and asked her how long she had had the problem: two years. Had anything happened at that time? Her son had cystic fibrosis and was in intensive care at the time fighting for his life. I said I felt she had perhaps taken on the burden of her son which only the Lord wanted to take from her. With her permission I asked the Holy Spirit to take the burden and bring His *shalom* (His rightful ordering and authority, His peace). She fell to the floor under the Spirit and rested a few moments. She got up and I asked about the shoulder pain. It had completely gone. We thanked and praised God. I also explained that she needed to keep giving the Lord her son, and rest in His peace and love.

Louise's story is a classic case of emotional and physical healing being clearly linked. Often forgiveness of others and self is needed to unlock emotional/inner and physical healing.

Gareth Owen, one of the leaders of The Gate, has developed a simple acrostic for inner or emotional healing.[52] There are Bible studies he has prepared in the appendix for groups to use in exploring this area.

Praying for Inner Healing
- **W**hat lie am I believing
- **A**sk for the truth
- **R**enounce the lie and receive the truth
- **M**ove forward

The model emphasises the ability and importance of believers taking responsibility for their own emotional health. We can indeed pray for our own healing in all areas. It focuses on the need for truth and right understanding. It is a working out of Paul's writing in Romans 12. Our transformation comes through the 'renewing' of our minds and thinking patterns.

> Therefore, I urge you, brothers and sisters, in view of God's mercy, to offer your bodies as a living sacrifice, holy and pleasing to God – this is your true and proper worship. Do not conform to the pattern of this world, but be transformed by the renewing of your mind. Then you will be able to test and approve what God's will is – his good, pleasing, and perfect will. (Romans 12:1-2)

Dr Caroline Leaf, a Christian neuro-scientist, has taught extensively on how we can train our minds to think differently and literally re-programme and renew our brains. This is a

---

52 This draws from Sozo Bethel teaching.

fascinating example of science 'catching up' with biblical teaching such as Paul in Philippians 4, and 2 Corinthians 10.

We demolish arguments and every pretension that sets itself up against the knowledge of God, and we take captive every thought to make it obedient to Christ. (2 Corinthians 10:5)

Finally, brothers and sisters, whatever is true, whatever is noble, whatever is right, whatever is pure, whatever is lovely, whatever is admirable – if anything is excellent or praiseworthy – think about such things. (Philippians 4:8)

The Bible teaches how we can take control of our thinking and our minds. This is a key part of gaining and sustaining healing for whole people.

Sometimes the Lord can supernaturally heal us on the inside. I had the privilege of going to the Bethel leader's advance for the first time in 2012. I remember we sang a song that was new to me at the time, 'God, I Look to You', many times over the few days I was there. (I also went for the Sunday evening before and visited the BSMM and healing rooms.)

God, I look to You, I won't be overwhelmed
Give me vision to see things like You do
God, I look to You, You're where my help comes from
Give me wisdom; You know just what to do

I will love You, Lord, my strength

Growing Together: Healing and Wholeness

I will love You, Lord, my shield
I will love You, Lord, my rock forever
All my days I will love You, God

Hallelujah our God reigns
Hallelujah our God reigns
Hallelujah our God reigns
Forever all my days, Hallelujah[53]

I found that every time we sang the song I cried! I did not understand why. At the end of the week, in the House of Prayer, I asked the Lord what was happening. I think it was then, but I became aware I no longer feared death in the same way. My view of death and spending eternity with the Lord had changed, especially as we had sung, 'Forever all my days, Hallelujah.' I believe the Lord had healed me of a fear of death, which has allowed me to walk more closely with Him. This was an interesting experience as it happened during worship and I was not aware of it at the time.

SPIRITUAL HEALING AND DELIVERANCE

Emotional and inner healing issues can create openings for spiritual attack and even demonic oppression. This can particularly include unforgiveness and taking offence. Other sources of spiritual/demonic oppression can include occult involvement, ungodly sexual activity, generational and other curses and unhealthy soul ties. Many leaders, even if they accept healing

---

53 *God, I Look to You*, written by Jenn Johnson and Ian McIntosh. Copyright © 2010 Bethel Music Publishing.

ministry, can be wary of deliverance. As C.S. Lewis[54] pointed out, we can sway between the twin extremes of dismissing demonic activity and thinking every problem is down to demonic attack. However, there are many clear cases in the Bible where Jesus cast out demons directly leading to physical healing.

Jesus was driving out a demon that was mute. When the demon left, the man who had been mute spoke, and the crowd was amazed. But some of them said, 'By Beelzebub, the prince of demons, he is driving out demons.' Others tested him by asking for a sign from heaven. Jesus knew their thoughts and said to them: 'Any kingdom divided against itself will be ruined, and a house divided against itself will fall. If Satan is divided against himself, how can his kingdom stand? I say this because you claim that I drive out demons by Beelzebub. Now if I drive out demons by Beelzebub, by whom do your followers drive them out? So then, they will be your judges. But if I drive out demons by the finger of God, then the kingdom of God has come upon you. When a strong man, fully armed, guards his own house, his possessions are safe. But when someone stronger attacks and overpowers him, he takes away the armour in which the man trusted and divides up his plunder. Whoever is not with me is against me, and whoever does not gather with me scatters. When an impure spirit comes out of a person, it goes through arid places seeking rest and does not find it. Then it says, "I will return to the house I left." When it arrives, it finds the house swept clean and put in order. Then it goes and takes seven other spirits more wicked than itself, and they go in and live there. And the final condition of that

---

54 C.S. Lewis, *Screwtape Letters* (HarperCollins, 2001).

person is worse than the first.' (Luke 11:14-26)

Jesus also makes clear in this passage the importance of building a stronghold of belief and love in a person after deliverance. It makes clear that we must work with people to help them build their understanding and spiritual strength and so this may be a process over time rather than some one-off event where we 'gain victory'. Obviously in a crusade or mission situation we often don't have the same choices as we may have in a local

Growing Together: Healing and Wholeness

church. Increasingly we also have other ministries[55] we can call on to help with difficult cases where some form of deliverance is thought to be needed but is beyond the current resources of the local church.

Based on this teaching we tend to propose that only Christians undergo deliverance. Or that someone is led to Christ as part of the process.

I recall being introduced to a man in a Brazilian church. Through the interpreter I was told the man was full of fear, especially of a skin condition he had. He said he had had a dream a year ago in which he saw me (!) set him free. At this stage I was aware everyone was watching me, and I was thinking is this a mental health issue or demonic oppression (or a mix of both)? After interviewing I found the man had been involved in a form of Brazilian witchcraft called *macumba* and that the man was not a Christian! He was quite happy to invite Jesus into his life. I then firmly but in a normal voice cast out the spirits of *macumba* and fear, and prayed for his physical healing. Finally, aware of Jesus' teaching above, I asked for the Holy Spirit to fill him. He fell on the floor seemingly full of the Spirit and peace.

All of this was via my translator as my Portuguese is not very good. Indeed, I recall him stopping me on one or two occasions as I was praying for people to be full of the Holy Spirit in what I thought was the right Portuguese (I thought I was saying, '*Vinde, Espírito Santo*', 'Come, Holy Spirit'). He told me what I was

---

55 For example, Ellel, Bethel Sozo and Restoring the Foundations.

saying made no sense! I said, 'Well, the Holy Spirit seems to understand', as people were being filled and falling under His presence!

A LOVING APPROACH TO DELIVERANCE

Many are wary of deliverance as a loud and messy affair. With the right loving approach and biblical teaching this is not usually necessary in my experience. I recommend the ten-step process of Pablo Bottari[56] as promulgated by Dr Randy Clark.[57] These steps are based on many years of experience and literally thousands of deliverances:

- **Step 1:** Make sure that the person is manifesting: we need with the Hoy Spirit's help to discern what might be causing a person's behaviour. Is it the Holy Spirit, demonic activity (Pablo distinguishes between a range of activity from oppression, through torment to demonisation/possession) or some form of mental illness, acting out, or personality disorder?
- **Step 2:** Take authority in the name of Jesus and bind the Spirit: we ensure the demon submits and so the person can be quiet, and we can communicate with them.
- **Step 3:** Bring to consciousness: we always need to help people take control of their bodies and minds, and cooperate in their deliverance.
- **Step 4:** Ask people if they want to be free. We can only

---

56 Pablo Bottari, *Free in Christ* (Charisma House, 2001).

57 Dr Randy Clark, *The Biblical Guidebook to Deliverance* (Charisma House, 2015),

really help people if they want to be free. They have to
cooperate with us and ask Jesus to bring them freedom.
If people are not yet ready, we still love them! We can help
them with teaching and encouragement, and ensure
they have ongoing pastoral care until they are ready.

- **Step 5:** Receive: Jesus Christ as Lord and Saviour who
  alone can bring freedom and in whose name we have
  authority.
- **Step 6:** Reveal: discovering the areas of bondage and open
  doors as a consequence of sin as the Holy Spirit leads us
  and in an atmosphere of love and non-judgement
  people share their stories.
- **Step 7:** Renounce: invite people to pray to renounce and
  break the causes of demonic oppression as they are revealed.
- **Step 8:** Rebuke: taking authority in the name of Jesus as
  they minister to break all ties and drive out all unclean
  spirits.
- **Step 9:** Rejoice: give thanks to God for deliverance.
  Leading people to thank Jesus for their freedom.
- **Step 10:** Rebuild, encouraging people to ask the Lord
  to fill them with the anointing, presence, power, and
  grace of the Holy Spirit.

In reality this process can be quite quick and not all the steps
are always needed. But in my and others' experience they do
greatly reduce the likelihood of a 'messy' deliverance that can
even cause concern and hurt for others. Above all we want to
love people through into freedom as we take the authority Jesus

Growing Together: Healing and Wholeness

has given us.

In May 2017, I was part of an Agape Team serving the Felhaz[58] student movement in Budapest. The final night was an outreach in the Akuarium nightclub in the centre of the city with many thousands of young people present. There were many prophetic words, healings, deliverances, salvations, and Holy Spirit impartations. Mid-way through the evening (which ended at 3am!), a young woman who the Lord had beautifully set free earlier in the week brought her brother, Tom, to me. She wanted me to pray for him.

It is always sensible to pray for deliverance in pairs or a small team with one person leading and others praying and discerning what's going on. My son, Adam, and I interviewed him. It turned out he had two badly busted elbows with pain and significant unusual movement. This had come from falling off a wall three years ago at a Christian camp and holding out his elbows to protect himself. His real problem however, he said, was that he was depressed and could see no point in living.

We decided to work through the original accident and associated issues. As we prayed we realised we had to deal with a spirit of trauma associated with the accident. This is an example of an 'open door'. We bound the spirit, led him to renounce it and cast it out in Jesus' name. Adam discerned other associated spirits including shame, abandonment, and depression. I led Tom through the deliverance process as Adam and Tom's sister prayed in support. We also encouraged Tom to forgive himself

---

58 *Felhaz* means Upper Room in Hungarian. It's an amazing move of God which started in 2015 with three passionate students. They now gather weekly with many hundreds and sometimes thousands of students and young people and flow regularly in the supernatural gifts of the Holy Spirit.

Finding freedom, by Jenny Whitfield

and any others involved. He said he felt much better and the feelings of unworthiness and depression had gone.

We then asked him about his elbows. These had begun to feel better – showing the link between spiritual oppression and physical healing. I encouraged Tom with the stories of other people's elbows we had seen healed just that week. We prayed again for his elbows – his pain went, and movement returned nearly to normal. This was quite a big deal to him as he was an amateur basketball player! We encouraged him to read the word and strengthen himself in the Lord. It's important to ensure an opposite godly stronghold of love, forgiveness, peace, etc. is built when people are delivered and set free. He and his sister left with big smiles!

MENTAL HEALTH

Mental health is as much on God's heart as physical and spiritual health. Peter Horrobin's definition that 'healing is the restoration of God's order to the spirit, soul and body' clearly implies healing and restoration of all aspects of mental illness. Mental health problems are often complex and hard to identify. Although much has changed there is still a stigma attached. Generally, we do not approach mental health issues as we do physical health.

Mental health issues are very common – generally one in four of the population will suffer from something during their life. In my own life I can immediately think of over twenty people from my extended family and friends who have suffered from a variety of issues including schizophrenia, bipolar, anxiety, depression, post-natal depression, post-traumatic stress disorder, alcoholism, drug addiction, dementia, autism, abuse, and suicide. The reasons are many and complex often involving some mix of genetic, biochemical, environmental, family, emotional, spiritual and at times demonic causes.

There are many examples of people with mental health issues in the Bible such as Elijah's 'depression' after the encounter with the prophets of Baal in 1 Kings 19:4. God's dealings with him demonstrate practical care (he was fed and watered) as well as a deeper revelation of his character and nature.

As with physical illness we need to encourage people to also work with healthcare professionals as well as receiving prayer. Counselling and psychotherapy can help people understand their issues and perhaps the roots of them. This can then help them ask for prayer and ministry to the root issues. Similarly, words of knowledge and revelatory gifts of the Spirit can also lead to significant inner healing.

I remember an old work colleague who the Lord healed of anxiety through a complex interplay of counselling, medication, inner healing, and deliverance, orchestrated as it were by the Holy Spirit. It was actually my first direct involvement with deliverance as one evening on an overseas business trip, he told me he was feeling unwell and asked if I would pray for him. The next moment he was rolling round the floor, growling and with his hands and fingers grasped tightly. I was pretty sure he was 'manifesting' a demonic spirit. Neither of us really understood what was happening at the time but I knew enough to bind the oppressing spirit. We sought more informed help

Growing Together: Healing and Wholeness

back home!

However, often people with mental health challenges are not healed quickly and fully. They must learn to walk into recovery and manage the pressures and stresses of life. We need to love, care for, and support each other. Many walk with such mental health 'limps' as Jacob walked with his limping hip in Genesis 32:22-32 after his encounter with God. If our churches are truly to become healing places for all, we should talk about mental health and illness. We should encourage people to be real and honest. This can be part of people's coping and healing too.

SUSTAINING HEALING

One of the sad challenges of the healing ministry is to see people 'lose' their healing. It is important, therefore, that we encourage and help people who have received healing. Key steps include:

- Helping people understand what's happened to them and how their thinking needs to change. We need to use opportunities for brief but critical biblical teaching to help underpin people's healing.
- Encourage people to read the Bible and key scriptures relating to their situation or more general healing scriptures such as Psalm 103.
- Ensure people are being discipled and part of a loving supportive small group and church.
- Encourage people to take authority to command any

pain or symptoms to leave if it returns. This is especially important if the cause is demonic or a spirit of affliction.

- Addressing (lovingly) any lifestyle issues that may be contributing to people's condition e.g. smoking and chest problems. I recall praying for three nights running for a young man with shoulder and neck pain. It left each time but came back as he crouched over his laptop each day, all day.

- Sometimes, this involves addressing wider circumstances and the environment. There is a person I have prayed for who, despite many hours of prayer, with healing at times, seems to always slip back into illness. I believe the Holy Spirit has prompted me to realise that until they were ready to move home, they'd be stuck in their current pattern.

GROWING IN WHOLENESS

In this chapter we have explored how any healing ministry needs to be balanced and integrated, addressing people as whole beings – body, mind, spirit, and relational. We have seen in my friends, Louise and Tom, how healing in the inmost being – in emotions, memories, thought, and spirit – can lead to healing in the body.

My encouragement is to learn to let the Holy Spirit lead and teach you as you meet people. Who can truly know a person and the roots of their wounds and hurts except God? Let us learn to walk with Jesus, the Great Physician!

9

THE INVITATION: KEYS TO GROWING IN HEALING

"We shall not cease from exploration and the end of all our exploring will be to arrive where we started and to know the place for the first time."

T.S. Eliot

Breaking through in the healing ministry can take a long time. Not surprisingly, overcoming years if not centuries of teaching that these gifts don't apply today, moving past personal fears and disappointments, and overcoming demonic resistance, is a challenge! Today increasingly many Christians and even whole churches in the West are breaking through. Healing is becoming anticipated rather than a rare longed-for event. Not guaranteed but perhaps common.

I believe the Lord is inviting churches of all types, sizes, and backgrounds into an adventure with Him in healing. So in this chapter I want to highlight a number of keys for churches along this journey, perhaps by now in stage 3, and for individuals pressing into healing. These, I believe, will increase the likelihood and scope of healing. They have come from studying the word,

The Invitation: Keys to Growing in Healing

and from reading, listening to, and watching some amazing women and men, and from my own experience.

The four keys are:

- **Identity**: being rooted and established in our identity as children of God and learning to live and minister from that deep truth in love and faith.
- **Intimacy**: seeking the presence of God and allowing Him to guide and teach us, whether we understand or not.
- **Impartation**: seeking and walking in faith and the anointing of God for healing.
- **Integrity**: walking in consistent truth, holiness, and gratitude.

KEY #1: IDENTITY

We need to be rooted in our identity as children of God

I have repeatedly found that being absolutely clear on my identity as a child of God is key to my whole walk with the Lord. And to anything I might do with Him, for Him, or in any form of 'ministry'. I remember during my five-day silent retreat in 2014, before the mission trip to Brazil, how to my surprise the Lord spent two days 'hammering' me with the truth of the words of Romans 8, and especially verse 17.

For those who are led by the Spirit of God are the children of God. The Spirit you received does not make you slaves, so that you live in fear again; rather, the Spirit you received brought about your adoption to sonship. And by him we cry, 'Abba, Father.' The Spirit himself testifies with our spirit that we are God's children. Now if we are children, then we are heirs – heirs of God and co-heirs with Christ, if indeed we share in his sufferings in order that we may also share in his glory. (Romans 8:14-17)

I had heard Canon Andrew White talk about the experience of Christians in Baghdad. He had referenced this verse. It would not get out of my head. I read it, meditated on it, painted it, and prayed it. Did I really believe I was a child of God? And an heir? A co-heir with Christ? Do you? Really, really know it and live from the truth of this?

So, when I come to pray with someone, I come knowing the authority I have because I'm His son. Not because of what I have done or can do. It does not depend on my good deeds, 'righteousness', or following a formula. As the song[59] goes, 'it's who I am' because of who He is; our good Father.

You're a good, good Father
It's who You are, it's who you are, it's who You are
And I'm loved by You
It's who I am, it's who I am, it's who I am

I have two sons and when they'd ask me for something, especially when they were little, like a hug or a kiss or to be thrown up in to air (no mean feat, if you've met either of them!), I'd not require a certain formula or perfect behaviour. I'd never doubt

---

59 *Good, Good Father* by Anthony Brown and Patrick Barrett. Copyright © 2014 Sixsteps Music/Vamos Publishing/worshiptogether.com songs/Capitol CMG Paragon/Common Hymnal Publishing/Housefires Sounds/Tony Brown Publishing Designee. Admin. by Integrity Music, Song Solutions.

The Invitation: Keys to Growing in Healing

for a second that I loved them completely and wanted the best for them. Do we believe this about us and Father God?

And the second part of verse 17 hit me: '*if* indeed we share in his sufferings in order that we may also share in his glory'. The 'If' stood out to me. Did I share His sufferings? How did I share His sufferings? How could I share His sufferings? I became, and still am, very clear that this 'sharing in His sufferings' was nothing to do with sickness. There really is no biblical case for considering sickness as generally God-sent.[60] No, it was clear that for the Roman Christians and Paul the suffering was persecution from witnessing and bringing the Kingdom.

For me, and most of us in the West today, there is mainly some (usually good natured) rejection from people when we share the gospel with them. Over the last year I guess I have had hundreds of people reject the basic gospel message. I can remember maybe three or four rude people in the whole year. Many, many more were thankful and grateful to be blessed even if they did not want to know more (and many also were keen to hear more and make a step towards knowing Jesus better).

I also realised that for me, for us, some of this 'suffering' might be from praying for healing and not seeing people healed immediately. Not really suffering like our Iraqi brothers and sisters! But there is a pain and suffering in seeing people not healed. If we want to share His glory, we need to be bold and share His gospel and offer healing prayer.

So, we need to fully know and own our identity as beloved

---

60 This is not to say God does not use suffering to refine, shape, and grow us. See *God on Mute* by Pete Greig for a sensitive and insightful exploration of the issues around suffering and unanswered prayer.

children of God. And we need to embrace and walk in the power (*dunamis*) and authority (*exousia*) He has given us (see Luke chapters 9 and 10, Matthew 28 and Mark 16 – Great Commissions).

This has also been one of the core teachings from The Turning. Often, before Christians can share their faith with strangers, they have to receive afresh this 'adoption' as children of God.[61]

As the saying goes, like father, like son. Jesus said:

Jesus gave them this answer: 'Very truly I tell you, the Son can do nothing by himself; he can do only what he sees his Father doing, because whatever the Father does the Son also does. For the Father loves the Son and shows him all he does.' (John 5:19-20a)

We, too, represent the Father now. Paul says we are ambassadors:

We are therefore Christ's ambassadors, as though God were making his appeal through us. (2 Corinthians 5:20)

I will never forget the instructions Dr Randy Clark gave us as his ministry team the first night in Brazil. I hardly had a clue what was happening or what to do. I was hoping for some know-how to be passed on. What he said though has stuck with me. Basically, he said, 'I don't mind if you pray and don't see anyone healed but I do want everyone you encounter to be loved.' If we are to walk and minister like Jesus, then we must

---

61 The powerful song by Jonathan Hesler, *No Longer Slaves,* is a great resource to assist in this.

love, because He is love. Often feeling compassion rise in us can also be a sign that the Father wants to heal.

KEY #2: INTIMACY – SEEKING GOD'S PRESENCE, AND LEARNING TO WALK IN DEPENDENCE AND FRIENDSHIP

Ultimately only the presence of God and empowering through the Holy Spirit can lead anyone to saving faith or to healing, deliverance, and freedom. We therefore need to learn as believers, as leaders, and as churches to seek the presence of God. It's vital for growing in personal and corporate intimacy. Corporate worship is a key aspect of this. From and in His presence, relationship grows.

As we have seen above, our authority is from relationship and so we need to seek greater intimacy and deeper relationship with Him because that is our heart's desire. And from these flow more authority and confidence. Thus, we can confront the enemy and his schemes with the Lord's power and authority He has vested in us. As John Paul Jackson taught, power is given but authority comes from relationship. Relationship does not change in one sense but in a much more meaningful sense it deepens and grows.

So, as we press more into Him so, too, He leads us in sanctification, in to deeper holiness and the closing of any doors or eradication of footholds the enemy can use to trip or divert us. And again, this strengthens our ministry as we learn about ourselves and our own brokenness and wounds, which He in turn heals.

The Invitation: Keys to Growing in Healing

Jesus called His first disciples 'friends'. Whilst we will always also walk in fear and awe of God, walking a child in deeper and deeper intimacy and reliance on Him is key to our growth and ministry.

You are my friends if you do what I command. I no longer call you servants, because a servant does not know his master's business. Instead, I have called you friends, for everything that I learned from my Father I have made known to you. (John 15:14-15)

Why should I worry if the king of a whole country, faced by the demands of leading a whole nation, could just let God be in control, as David did in Psalm 131.

My heart is not proud, Lord, my eyes are not haughty; I do not concern myself with great matters or things too wonderful for me. But I have calmed and quietened myself, I am like a weaned child with its mother; like a weaned child I am content. Israel, put your hope in the Lord both now and for evermore. (Psalm 131)

As we have seen, Jesus said that He only did what He saw the Father doing. We need to learn to be led by Him. Words of knowledge, a feeling of compassion rising or, for some, feeling certain physical manifestations,[62] can be signs that He wants to heal.

Sometimes I have seen others or myself ask someone to do something and thought, 'Where did that come from?' This

---

62 For me it's usually warmth/gentle shaking of one hand/arm but it varies for people – and often there are no physical signs when the Lord begins to move in healing.

can be a word of knowledge or another way in which the Holy Spirit is guiding us.

In 2016 I had opportunity to share the testimony of a lady with MS receiving healing (at least from all her symptoms at the time) as I was preaching. At the end of the service a lady came up, very slowly, supported by a stick. She had to sit down. Violet was in her mid-thirties but had had MS for many years and was in great pain. I asked a friend to join me in praying for her with another lady from the church.

We shared again the testimony of the lady with MS healed to help build her faith. We then prayed again for her pain to go and strength to return. Nothing appeared to be happening as we re-interviewed her. As we prayed for her, I felt the Holy Spirit say to ask her to do something she could not easily do. I asked her to stand up. I think on reflection this may have been a word of knowledge as it wasn't my usual practice (though I had heard it taught).

She told me I was not her friend and was cruel to her. She tried to stand up as she did normally as taught by her physio. Then, suddenly, she said, 'I can do this,' and stood up. As we kept praying for her in tongues she walked up and down the room with no cane, getting increased freedom. She became free in movement and very excited. We were by her side and just thanking Jesus.

She stepped on to the stage, a small step. She asked if we had any stairs, as she couldn't do stairs. We opened the doors, so she could walk up the stairs to the church office. She was very excited as she did this freely. She kept telling us she could not normally do this.

We encouraged her to walk out her healing and take authority over it.

Alas, when I next had contact with her she had lost some of her freedom, and symptoms had returned at least in part. We prayed again for her with some small gain. Later I met a close friend of hers, who explained to me that they were a Christian and 'believed God could heal, but . . .' and then effectively explained how they did not believe in healing now. They had told their friend her 'healing' was just psychological! As we chatted, I realised part of her challenge was her friend's unbelief and resistance.

This is another example of our integrated nature and sometimes, therefore, the complexity of our healing journey.

KEY #3: IMPARTATION – RECEIVE IMPARTATION, CARRY ANOINTING, AND GROW IN FAITH

Whilst all the above are true and helpful, there is also a clear biblical basis for impartation of spiritual gifts including gifts of words of knowledge, discernment, healing, and working of miracles. I would therefore encourage leaders to seek impartation from people with recognised gifting. Dr Randy Clark is well known for this gifting and has written a very helpful book on the biblical background.[63] I have certainly received powerful impartations from Dr Randy and others.

---

63 Dr Randy Clark, *There is More* (Chosen Books, 2013).

He said to them, 'Go into all the world and preach the gospel to all creation. Whoever believes and is baptised will be saved, but whoever does not believe will be condemned. And these signs will accompany those who believe: in my name they will drive out demons; they will speak in new tongues . . . they will place their hands on people who are ill, and they will get well.' (Mark 16:15-18)

Sometimes the Lord uses times of impartation, too, to do other work. I recall in Budapest that another team member taught on words of knowledge and asked me to then give an impartation to everyone as they left the meeting. One lady, as I took her hand and asked the Holy Spirit to impart gifts of healing to her, fell to the floor under the Spirit. After everyone else had been through, I spoke with her and her husband. This was all new to them. But it turned out she had a real heartache and yearning for healing because they had a baby born with an abnormal head. I believe the Lord had met her in her hunger.

As we prayed for her and her husband he also started vibrating! His whole body shook! I understood this was his body turning in to the heartbeat of Father God. I encouraged them both to pray for their daughter even as she slept and release the *shalom* of God over her (as taught by Chris Gore of Bethel). They left encouraged.

And God has placed in the church first of all apostles, second prophets, third teachers, then miracles, then gifts of healing, of helping, of guidance, and of different kinds of tongues. Are all apostles? Are all prophets? Are all teachers? Do all work miracles? Do all have

Trusting, by Jenny Whitfield.

gifts of healing? Do all speak in tongues? Do all interpret? Now eagerly desire the greater gifts. (1 Corinthians 12:28-31)

I understand that the Bible teaches that all believers are to share the gospel and pray for healing. We can all pray and see people healed. This is an expectation we can set in our churches. But clearly it is also true that different people will have different ministries and gifts. These will vary in respect of healing too. Thus, there is also an anointing for healing which people carry, and which can grow as people seek the Lord and receive further impartation.

I often hear people say, 'I have prayed for people to be healed. Nothing happened.' I ask how many people have you prayed for? And how many times each?

Todd White's testimony is encouraging in this respect in that he reckons he prayed for over seven hundred people until he saw someone healed! He admittedly really went for it so saw these 'failures' in just a few months. His wife refused to go food shopping with him anymore! And then one day someone was healed. And then another, and another. All heaven has broken out in his ministry.

What Todd and many others teach us is to keep pressing in, to keep going for it, until we see breakthrough. Yes, we can learn more and we can seek impartation but there is no substitute for pressing through. Sometimes praying and fasting can help us sharpen ourselves in our reliance on the Lord. But there's no formula!

Jesus clearly taught that faith was critical to healing. We can think that faith is like putting the plug in the wall. It connects the need to the power source. But we must always remember that the Lord is the power source. Jesus has done the work on the cross as Isaiah 53 reminds us. Faith grabs hold of this and relies on it, as His fellow co-heirs of the Kingdom.

> 'Have faith in God,' Jesus answered. 'Truly I tell you, if anyone says to this mountain, "Go, throw yourself into the sea," and does not doubt in their heart but believes that what they say will happen, it will be done for them. Therefore I tell you, whatever you ask for in prayer, believe that you have received it, and it will be yours.' (Mark 11:22-24)

We need to remember it is faith *in Him* which is critical, not our faith per se. Indeed, sometimes the Lord gives gifts of faith as described in 1 Corinthians 12, where we 'know but know' He is going to work. We have the faith *of* God in these situations.

Francis MacNutt and Dr Randy Clark have both written specifically and helpfully on faith relating to healing. So, it is useful if we can grow our own faith and those of people we are leading and praying with. Helpful ways to do this include:

- Teaching on healing

Illustrating and explaining, especially from Jesus' life and Acts, about healing helps build an understanding and expectation.

- Testimonies and sharing stories of what God has done

The Invitation: Keys to Growing in Healing

Sometimes just sharing what Jesus has done releases the power for it to happen again. Revelation 19 points to this: '*For the testimony of Jesus is the spirit of prophecy*' (Revelation 19:10b NKJV).

This is also why if someone is healed of a particular condition and others have it, we can encourage them to pray for people. At a healing seminar in 2016 we did this and set off an amazing chain of healing where it seemed eighty per cent of the twenty or so people in the seminar received healing!

- Showing videos of healings

I remember praying with a team of people and Dr Randy Clark for a woman at a conference in Southampton who had a metal plate in her neck which gave her restricted movement and pain. As we prayed he showed her videos of people being healed of metal-related injuries and chronic pain. As we watched, and we prayed, all the pain went and she regained eighty per cent of her movement. She was amazed!

Dr Randy often shows videos of prior healings in his meetings. Many people are healed just watching the video, especially where they understand how faith and healing works!

- Declaring what God is doing

As we learn to perceive what the Father wants to do and indeed is doing in a meeting, we can increase faith by speaking it out. There is power in our words and positive affirmation can build faith (but not hype). Bill Johnson speaks of his experience that

The Invitation: Keys to Growing in Healing

when he says at the start of a meeting that it is normal for people to be healed in worship, they are. When he does not, it's much less likely.

KEY #4: INTEGRITY – TRUTH FROM THE INSIDE OUT

Paul in Ephesians 6 teaches about the importance of prayer, perseverance, and spiritual warfare in standing against Satan and his works. These are critical lessons for growing in the healing ministry.

> *Finally, be strong in the Lord and in his mighty power. Put on the full armour of God, so that you can take your stand against the devil's schemes. For our struggle is not against flesh and blood, but against the rulers, against the authorities, against the powers of this dark world and against the spiritual forces of evil in the heavenly realms. Therefore put on the full armour of God, so that when the day of evil comes, you may be able to stand your ground, and after you have done everything, to stand. Stand firm then, with the belt of truth buckled round your waist, with the breastplate of righteousness in place, and with your feet fitted with the readiness that comes from the gospel of peace. In addition to all this, take up the shield of faith, with which you can extinguish all the flaming arrows of the evil one. Take the helmet of salvation and the sword of the Spirit, which is the word of God. And pray in the Spirit on all occasions with all kinds of prayers and requests. (Ephesians 6:10-18)*

Paul exhorts us to live as people of truth, faith, righteousness, peace, the Spirit, and consistent and persistent prayer. Undergirding it all is his exhortation in verse 14 to stand firm with the 'belt of truth'. For the Roman soldiers, upon whom Paul was basing his description, the belt was an unseen but critical piece of equipment, on which his weapons could be hung and which kept his tunic in place so he could move and advance. For Christians this is a powerful picture of integrity, which is 'truth from the inside out'. Integrity is unseen yet critical to our walk and growth in the Lord.

From the sweep of scripture there is an apparent link between holiness and healing. In Exodus, the self-revelation of God as the healer-God is linked to obedience to His laws and ways.

> He said, 'If you listen carefully to the LORD your God and do what is right in his eyes, if you pay attention to his commands and keep all his decrees, I will not bring on you any of the diseases I brought on the Egyptians, for I am the LORD, who heals you.' (Exodus 15:26)

We see this repeated in many stories throughout scripture. Generally, people are more likely to be healed if there is no unconfessed sin in the person praying or the person or their family receiving prayer. Yet the story of Job illustrates that even godly people can experience inexplicable and unfathomable pain and suffering. Job lost his possessions, family, and health. God Himself said of Job that,

> 'There is no one on earth like him; he is blameless and upright, a man who fears God and shuns evil.' (Job 1:8)

Through the Book of Job we see a wrestle and struggle by Job's friends and Job himself, to make sense of Job's suffering. Job hangs on to his integrity and faith. In the end he encounters the Lord and all His might, majesty, and transcendence. Job is 'content' to rest in awe of the majesty and mystery of God.

> *'Surely I spoke of things I did not understand, things too wonderful for me to know. You said, "Listen now, and I will speak; I will question you, and you shall answer me." My ears had heard of you but now my eyes have seen you. Therefore I despise myself and repent in dust and ashes.' (Job 42:3b-6)*

A number of the people I have known who have died before their time were the most holy and faithful. They usually had the sort of 'but even if' faith of the Bible. This was the faith of young Israelites kidnapped by Babylon.

> *Shadrach, Meshach and Abednego replied to him, 'King Nebuchadnezzar, we do not need to defend ourselves before you in this matter. If we are thrown into the blazing furnace, the God we serve is able to deliver us from it, and he will deliver us from Your Majesty's hand.* **But even if he does not***, we want you to know, Your Majesty, that we will not serve your gods or worship the image of gold you have set up.' (Daniel 3:16-18 emphasis added)*

This was the faith of friends who loved Jesus dearly, believed fervently in the power of healing prayer, and faced death squarely with courage. They knew they were going to be with Jesus and yet knew they were leaving their grieving families. They were the most holy and faithful, the most trusting and pure. There is no simple equation.

So, we should confess our sins as per James 5, but we cannot simplistically relate unanswered prayer and sin.

> *Therefore confess your sins to each other and pray for each other so that you may be healed. The prayer of a righteous person is powerful and effective. (James 5:16)*

It seems clear from the Bible that sickness and disease entered into the world because of the fall and sin. Sometimes a connection with sin and sickness might be obvious, as in Genesis 12 when Pharaoh took Abram's wife Sarai as his own because of Abram's deceit. We also see Jesus forgive sins as part of His healing ministry.

However, elsewhere in Jesus' ministry we see Him confirm a man was born blind not because of his or his parent's sin.

> *As he went along, he saw a man blind from birth. His disciples asked him, 'Rabbi, who sinned, this man or his parents, that he was born blind?' 'Neither this man nor his parents sinned,' said Jesus, 'but this happened so that the works of God might be displayed in him.' (John 9:1-4)*

Jesus said it was 'so that the works of God might be displayed in him'. Frankly we often don't know why things are as they are. And Jesus exhorted us in Matthew 7 not to judge. We always need to stay non-judgemental in the healing ministry.

We also benefit hugely from the power of celebrating the Lord's Supper in Communion, Eucharist, or Mass. Deliberately bringing ourselves in repentance under the power of the cross and Christ's shed blood is important to our walk and health.

> *For I received from the Lord that which I also delivered to you: that the Lord Jesus on the same night in which He was betrayed took bread; and when He had given thanks, He broke it and said, 'Take, eat; this is My body which is broken for you; do this in remembrance of Me.' In the same manner He also took the cup after supper, saying, 'This cup is the new covenant in My blood. This do, as often as you drink it, in remembrance of Me.' For as often as you eat this bread and drink this cup, you proclaim the Lord's death till He comes. (1 Corinthians 11:23-26 NKJV)*

But it is God who heals. Clearly people with obvious sin in their lives get healed – thank God! And He uses us in all our imperfection and fallenness! Jesus came for those who needed help and knew it!

It is often helpful and sometimes prompted by the Holy Spirit to ask people to confess their sins. This is especially in respect of any unforgiveness. Jesus was very clear about the necessity for and power of forgiveness. We suffer if we do not release forgiveness and this can create a foothold for the enemy. This can lead to a whole stronghold of unforgiveness, offence, and bitterness.

The Invitation: Keys to Growing in Healing

For if you forgive other people when they sin against you, your heavenly Father will also forgive you. But if you do not forgive others their sins, your Father will not forgive your sins. (Matthew 6:14-15)

In Rodney Hogue's very useful book *Forgiveness,* he not only talks through how people can be helped to forgive others but how important it is to then build a positive stronghold of love and compassion in place of bitterness and offence.

Finally under this key of integrity and truth, I think it is vital to remember that in our twenty-first-century world as children of the enlightenment and 'rational scientific thought' there can be an underlying belief that 'everything' can be explained. And if we can't explain it, it may not be real. This is pretty much the line of argument that secular humanist thinking and Christian liberal and cessationist thinking ends up with.

For my original career I wanted to be a research scientist, a developmental molecular biologist. I recall the excitement of my college director of studies, Dr Tim Hunt, the recently infamous but actually a really good bloke, telling me all about his summer discoveries about RNA expression in 1985 at Woods Hole, USA. He won a Nobel Prize for this subsequently. So, I had plenty of modernist scientific education.

It is clearly not true that we can explain everything. Just consider concepts like beauty, love, and altruism. As I said in the Introduction, we must have room for mystery, especially regarding God!

This is especially true about when, why, and how people get healed or don't. We must choose to trust God. He is good, utterly good. He is good in a way that is beyond our understanding. He defines 'good', not us. So, I trust Him and choose to keep persevering.

I mentioned before the concept of a 'mystery box' that I imagine by my side and into which I put those things I don't understand. My God is big enough for any and all mysteries. As I press in for more I may understand more of why people might not be healed and what I could do differently. But I will never know enough to satisfy my rational mind. But I know who my Father is, and I trust Him.

OUR INVITATION TO A JOURNEY

I believe the Lord's commission to His disciples in Luke 10 still calls us into a life of mission as individual believers and the church, His body.

> He told them, 'The harvest is plentiful, but the workers are few. Ask the Lord of the harvest, therefore, to send out workers into his harvest field . . . Heal those there who are ill and tell them, "The kingdom of God has come near to you."' (Luke 10:2, 9)

The 'harvest', both in need and opportunity, is as great as during Jesus' earthly ministry. He invites us all – regardless of church denomination, type, size, experience, or stream, into an adventure with Him in healing. As I was finishing this book, I was having an interview for a role serving a network of churches and was wondering if the role might detract from my own journey in healing. As I sat with one of the other candidates waiting for our turn, we struck up a conversation. I saw him fiddling with his thumb and soon discovered it was very painful and had come on that morning. After asking his permission I prayed for healing and he reported all the pain was gone! I took the hint!

The Lord has commissioned us to proclaim and demonstrate the Kingdom of God, and to teach all nations to be His disciples and to do as He did! It's an invitation to a journey of adventure and learning. It will be full of amazing stories of hope and rejoicing but also sadness and frustration. Are we up for 'sharing his suffering' that we might also 'share in his glory'?[64] He has shown us the way and, what He calls us to, He will equip us for.

Will you accept His invitation?

---

64 'Now if we are children, then we are heirs – heirs of God and co-heirs with Christ, if indeed we share in his sufferings in order that we may also share in his glory.' (Romans 8:17)

RESOURCES

"Don't let small minds convince you that your dreams are too big."

Kathryn Kuhlman

Link to online Gate messages:

Visit http://www.thegate.uk.com/Archived-Sermons/ to find most of the following messgaes – use the search function using the given Topic to find the message.

TOPIC	SPEAKER	LINK
Isaiah 61 His Story Our Story the Whole Story	Alastair Mitchell-Baker	isaiah-61-his-story-our-story-the-whole-story/
Overcoming Demonic Powers	Yinka Oyekan	overcoming-demonic-powers/
Avoiding Demonic Landing Trips	Yinka Oyekan	avoiding_demonic_landing_strips/
Isaiah 61 How You Can Join In	Danni Malone and Jeremy Sharpe	isaiah-61-how-can-you-join-in/
Our Commission to Heal	Alastair Mitchell-Baker	our-commission-to-heal/
Words of Knowledge	Yinka Oyekan	words-of-knowledge/
Healing	Yinka Oyekan	healing-yinka-26th-march/
Praying for Inner Healing 1	Gareth Owen	http://thegate.uk.com/preacher/gareth-owen/
Praying for Inner Healing 2	Gareth Owen	http://thegate.uk.com/preacher/gareth-owen/
Inner Healing at Easter	Yinka Oyekan	easter-sunday-inner-healing/
Inner Healing	Yinka Oyekan	yinka-inner-healing/
Overcoming Disappointment	Alastair Mitchell-Baker	overcoming-disappointment/
Healthy Relationships	Yinka Oyekan	healthy-relationships/
Mental Health	Danni Malone	god-cares-for-your-mental-health/
Intimacy	Jo Moody	jo-moody-intimacy/

Resources

Faith and Grace in Action	Jo Moody	jo-moody-faith-and-grace-in-action/
Healing in His Shadow	Yinka Oyekan	healing-in-his-shadow/
Healing Communities	Alastair Mitchell-Baker	healing-communities/
Healing Our Communities	Yinka Oyekan	healing-our-communities/
Healing Communities	Danni Malone	healing-communities-2/
Healing	Julian Richards	healing/ (including how to pray for people who are not yet Christians/outside the church)
Being a Healthy Community	Yinka Oyekan	healing/
A Healthy Marriage	Yinka Oyekan	a-healthy-marriage/
The Power of Purity	Gareth Owen	the-power-of-purity/
The Healing Power of Saying No	Danni Malone	the-healing-power-of-saying-no/
Learning to Overcome	Alastair Mitchell-Baker	the-s-words-learning-to-overcome/

Resources

Recommended books and public domain talks and videos.

WEBSITES:
https://globalawakening.com/
http://www.agapefreedomfighters.org

BOOKS:
General healing ministry
The Bible
Ministry Team Training Manual – Randy Clark
Biblical Basis for Healing –Randy Clark
Essential Healing – Randy Clark and Bill Johnson
Doing Healing – Alexander Venter
Healing – Francis MacNutt
The Healing Breakthrough – Randy Clark
Walking in Supernatural Healing Power – Chris Gore

Physical healing
Essential Guide to Healing – Bill Johnson and Randy Clark
Healing Unplugged – Bill Johnson and Randy Clark

Inner healing and deliverance
Our Hands His Healing – Jeannie Morgan
Let the Healing Begin – Jeannie Morgan
Restoring the Foundation – Chester and Betty Kylstra
Forgiveness – Rodney Hogue
Free in Christ – Pablo Bottari
Healing and Deliverance – Peter Horrobin
Biblical Basis for Deliverance – Randy Clark
Finding Victory When Healing Doesn't Happen – Randy Clark and Craig Miller
Keep Your Love On – Danny Silk

Intimacy and relationship with God
When Heaven Invades Earth – Bill Johnson
Hosting the Presence – Bill Johnson
Supernatural Ways of Royalty – Kris Valloton
God on Mute – Pete Greig

Resources

Personal Transformation: Christ in Us – Yinka Oyekan
The Way of Blessing – Roy Godwin with Dave Roberts

Prophecy and listening to God
Translating God – Shawn Bolz
Hearing God – Brad Jersak

Impartation
There is More! – Randy Clark

Biography
God's Generals – Roberts Liardon
Minute by Minute – Jo Moody
Almighty is His Name (Sophal Ung) – Randy Clark and Susan Thompson

Resources

The following pages contain the notes from a five-week training seminar that was run at The Gate during 2017. I include them in the hope that you might find them useful in running your own training courses/seminars.

The Extravagant Father, by Sam Horne

The Gate Core Teaching Series
April to May, 2017

HEALING

The Spirit of the Lord is on me, because he has anointed me to proclaim good news to the poor. He has sent me to proclaim freedom for the prisoners and recovery of sight for the blind, to set the oppressed free, to proclaim the year of the Lord's favour.
Luke 4

KEY TO USING THE STUDY NOTES

These notes have been prepared for you to use either in small groups, as teaching material, or for your own personal study times. They are designed to be flexible, giving you the opportunity to think, discuss and pray about what God might be saying.

PREPARATION AND REVIEW

The Preparation and Review sections are designed to give you or your group members a challenge at the end of each session. They are really important practical exercises.

Please ensure that you review how everyone got on at the start of the next session. If you are not sure that you will cover all the material in the time available, make sure you finish each session with the **Preparation**, ready for next time.

ⓧ Individual study: suitable for personal study in your own time.

⚙ Practical ideas: suggested exercise or idea that might help understanding.

💬 Group discussion: suitable for small groups to discuss.

📖 Bible quotation. All scriptures in this guide use the NIV.

🌐 Supplementary questions: this is going a little deeper.

HEALING – GETTING STARTED

REVIEW

💬 How has your understanding of God's heart for healing changed over the last 3 months?

We've been looking at healing on Sunday mornings for the last few weeks. These notes are designed to help you grow in your understanding and confidence in praying for healing.

📖 Read Luke 4:14-21, Jesus' so-called 'manifesto':

Jesus returned to Galilee in the power of the Spirit, and news about him spread through the whole countryside. He was teaching in their synagogues, and everyone praised him. He went to Nazareth, where he had been brought up, and on the Sabbath day he went into the synagogue, as was his custom. He stood up to read, and the scroll of the prophet Isaiah was handed to him. Unrolling it, he found the place where it is written:

"The Spirit of the Lord is on me,
because he has anointed me
to proclaim good news to the poor.

Healing – Getting Started

He has sent me to proclaim freedom for the prisoners
and recovery of sight for the blind,
to set the oppressed free,
to proclaim the year of the Lord's favour."

Then he rolled up the scroll, gave it back to the attendant and sat
down. The eyes of everyone in the synagogue were fastened on
him. He began by saying to them, "Today this scripture is fulfilled
in your hearing."

💬 **Jesus quotes this passage from Isaiah 61. What do you think this meant to his original hearers?**

```


```

💬 **And what does it mean for us?**

```


```

As a church we understand that Jesus passed this 'manifesto' or commission on to his disciples. And hence on to us. Read Luke 9:1-6 and Luke 10:1-9.

Healing – Getting Started

💬 What did Jesus tell his disciples to do in Luke 9 and 10?

💬 What happened?

📖 *Then Jesus came to them and said, "All authority in heaven and on earth has been given to me. Therefore go and make disciples of all nations, baptizing them in the name of the Father and of the Son and of the Holy Spirit, and teaching them to obey everything I have commanded you. And surely, I am with you always, to the very end of the age." Matthew 28*

💬 What was Jesus' commission to the disciples and what is it to us? What does this include?

Healing – Getting Started

📖 *He said, "If you listen carefully to the Lord your God and do what is right in his eyes, if you pay attention to his commands and keep all his decrees, I will not bring on you any of the diseases I brought on the Egyptians, for I am the Lord, who heals you." Exodus 15:26*

💬 **The name of God here is Jehovah-Rapha, God the Healer. What does this passage tell us about healing?**

📖 *Surely, he took up our pain and bore our suffering,*
yet we considered him punished by God,
   stricken by him, and afflicted.
But he was pierced for our transgressions,
   he was crushed for our iniquities;
the punishment that brought us peace was on him,
   and by his wounds we are healed. Isaiah 53:4-5

Healing – Getting Started

💬 What does this passage tell us about the basis for healing and the cross?

```
┌─────────────────────────────────────────────┐
│                                             │
│                                             │
│                                             │
│                                             │
│                                             │
│                                             │
└─────────────────────────────────────────────┘
```

💬 What other biblical bases are there for healing?

```
┌─────────────────────────────────────────────┐
│                                             │
│                                             │
│                                             │
│                                             │
└─────────────────────────────────────────────┘
```

PRAYING FOR HEALING

Hear from the person and the Holy Spirit
Exercise faith by praying (command/ask)
Ask what's happening
Love, affirm, and encourage

A simple model for praying for healing

💬 Have you tried this? What happened and what have you learnt?

⚙️ PRACTISING

In small groups ask who needs healing and practise using the model to pray for healing.

PRAYING FOR HEALING

REVIEW

💬 Have you had a chance to pray for someone for healing? What happened?

We want to learn more about how healing works, including how God uses Words of Knowledge, and how we can see more healing. It's important too that we talk about what happens when people do not get healed and how we deal with the disappointment and pain.

📖 *He gave them power and authority to drive out all demons and to cure diseases, and he sent them out to proclaim the kingdom of God and to heal the sick. Luke 9*

💬 What did Jesus give his disciples that enabled them to heal?

💬 **If Jesus has told us to heal people, do we need to ask him to heal people? Why?**

[blank box]

⚙ Generally, we encourage you to use simple 'command' prayers when praying for people. However, sometimes the Holy Spirit will lead you to use 'petition' or asking prayers. We can try these when command prayers don't seem to work. Can you think of examples in the Bible of command and asking prayers for healing?

[blank box]

Words of Knowledge are supernatural revelations of knowledge by the Holy Spirit. They are 'rhema' of God indicating his 'now,' in the moment intention and power to heal specific conditions, illnesses, or diseases. They contain within them the power and ability to bring the healing or miracle required. There is power in God's Word(s).

Praying for Healing

📖 *Then they came to Jericho. As Jesus and his disciples, together with a large crowd, were leaving the city, a blind man, Bartimaeus (which means "son of Timaeus"), was sitting by the roadside begging. When he heard that it was Jesus of Nazareth, he began to shout, "Jesus, Son of David, have mercy on me!" Many rebuked him and told him to be quiet, but he shouted all the more, "Son of David, have mercy on me!" Jesus stopped and said, "Call him." So, they called to the blind man, "Cheer up! On your feet! He's calling you." Throwing his cloak aside, he jumped to his feet and came to Jesus. "What do you want me to do for you?" Jesus asked him. The blind man said, "Rabbi, I want to see." "Go," said Jesus, "your faith has healed you." Immediately he received his sight and followed Jesus along the road. Mark 10*

💬 **A word of knowledge to us is like Jesus saying I want to heal you? How was this expressed to Bartimaeus?**

⚙️ How does the passage fit our simple model of praying for healing?

God want to speak to us. As his children we can be confident we can hear from him. There at least 7 different ways in which

words of knowledge can be given by the Holy Spirit:
- Pain or sensation in part of body
- Impression
- Picture of word
- (fleeting or short) Vision
- Open vision
- Dream
- Hearing

💬 **What biblical examples can you think of?**

```


```

💬 **What experience have you had giving or responding to words of knowledge?**

```


```

John Wimber said faith is spelt R-I-S-K. He prayed for hundreds if not thousands of people before anyone was healed. Dealing with disappointment is critical. We see people healed but not always. We must learn to cope with that. Watch a clip on YouTube

Praying for Healing

from Bill Johnson at **youtube.com/watch?v=ydmhYHCQgUM** (or search 'Bill Johnson on Disappointment'). Remember, Bill's own dad died from cancer when he was believing for Bethel to become a 'cancer free zone'.

💬 **What experience have you had with seeing people not healed? How did you feel?**

💬 **Have you worked through your disappointment? Have you given the Lord an 'offering' of praise even in your disappointment and pain?**

💬 The more people we pray for the more we will see healed. How can we encourage each other to pray for healing despite our disappointments?

⚙ PRACTISING

In your group ask the Holy Spirit for words of knowledge. Share what you receive – even if you are unsure – and pray for one another. Over the next week, ask the Lord to give you words of knowledge and see what happens! Share these whether at church or with people and offer to pray for the

EMOTIONAL HEALING

REVIEW

💬 How has your journey into praying for healing for people gone? What have you found exciting/what have you found challenging?

We've been looking at healing on Sunday mornings for the last couple of months. These notes are designed to help you grow in your understanding of how to enter wholeness in the realm of your emotions.

📖 Read Acts 3:1-8

One-day Peter and John were going up to the temple at the time of prayer – at three in the afternoon. Now a man who was lame from birth was being carried to the temple gate called Beautiful, where he was put every day to beg from those going into the temple courts. When he saw Peter and John about to enter, he asked them for money. Peter looked straight at him, as did John. Then Peter said, "Look at us!" So the man gave them his attention, expecting to get something from them. Then Peter said, "Silver or gold I do not have, but what I do have I give you.

In the name of Jesus Christ of Nazareth, walk." Taking him by the right hand, he helped him up, and instantly the man's feet and ankles became strong. He jumped to his feet and began to walk. Then he went with them into the temple courts, walking and jumping, and praising God.

This passage tells us that people can be made completely whole, all in the same moment. The man walked (he was physically healed, he jumped for joy (he was emotionally healed, and he went into the temple praising God (he was spiritually healed).

💬 **Do we believe that it is possible for us to see this happen?**

💬 **Have you got any testimonies of yourself or other people become whole as they met with God? What was this like?**

The most important thing we can do is step into the truth about ourselves.

Emotional Healing

📖 *My son, pay attention to what I say;*
turn your ear to my words.
Do not let them out of your sight,
keep them within your heart;
for they are life to those who find them
and health to one's whole body. Proverbs 4:20-22

💬 **What is God telling us in these verses in Proverbs? What effect does the Word of God have on us?**

⚙️ The Scripture asks us to do four things

1. Give God's word unrestricted access to our whole being. Let it permeate our lives.
2. Incline your ear – act of humility – this is the opposite of being proud and stiff-necked.
3. Do not let them depart from your eyes – if we keep one eye on the word and one eye on the world. Smith Wigglesworth said, "The trouble with many Christians is they have a spiritual squint. They are keeping one eye on the promises of God and one in other directions."
4. Keep them in the midst of your heart – if we keep God's word flowing through both the ear and the eye, it

will occupy our hearts.

The word is both Logos (What is in Scripture) and Rhema (a new utterance from God, Prophetic etc).

There is a lot in this to think about and meditate on. Use the rest of the session to talk as a group about how you apply these principles to your lives. Do you do these things?

WEEK 4

I CAN SET MYSELF FREE!

REVIEW

💬 How have you done with applying the principles from Proverbs 4 to your daily life?

📖 *Therefore, if anyone is in Christ they are a new Creation, Behold the old has gone and the new has come. 2 Corinthians 5:17*

📖 *Now a slave has no permanent place in the family, but a son belongs to it forever. So, if the Son sets you free you will be free indeed. John 8:35-36*

💬 The truth contained in 2 Corinthians 5 is powerful. How much do you believe it about your own life?

💬 The truth from John 8 is that Jesus has fully set us free. We are now longer slaves but sons and daughters. How much do

I Can Set Myself Free!

you believe this about your own life?

⚙ There are things that will stop us from being able to step into the truth about ourselves.

THERE ARE ISSUES IN OUR LIVES THAT WE'VE NOT RESOLVED

If we look at the life of Peter, there were issues in his life that were unresolved. He was obviously a fearless and impulsive person; he was the one that got out of the boat and walked on the water.

He was a leader amongst the disciples. He was also the one that drew his sword on the night that Jesus was betrayed and cut off the ear of this soldier. He was central to many of the arguments that the disciples had about who was the greatest. There was an issue with pride in him.

This meant that when Jesus was betrayed, and Peter was tested he failed.

📖 *But he gives us more grace. That is why Scripture says: 'God opposes the proud but shows favour to the humble.' Submit yourselves, then, to God. Resist the devil, and he will flee from you. James 4:6-7*

I Can Set Myself Free!

If we resist the Devil, the scripture tells us he, will flee from us but this must be done from a posture of humility. Have a think about Jesus's encounter with Satan in Matthew 4.

💬 **How did Jesus 'resist the devil'**

⚙️ *"In regard to the battlefield of the mind it is most helpful to spend the day developing godly virtues than to spend the day praying against the devil."* Francis Frangipane

💬 **What is a 'virtue' and how can we develop 'godly virtues'?**

WEEK 5

EMOTIONAL BEINGS

REVIEW

💬 How have you done in developing Godly Virtues in your life. Has this increased humility in you?

God has made us emotional beings. We are made in his image.

📖 *The Lord appeared to him from afar, saying, "I have loved you with an everlasting love; Therefore, I have drawn you with loving kindness". Jeremiah 31:3*

📖 *The Lord did not set His love on you nor choose you because you were more in number than any of the peoples, for you were the fewest of all peoples, but because the Lord loved you and kept the oath which he swore to your forefathers, the Lord brought you out by a mighty hand and redeemed you from the house of slavery, from the hand of Pharaoh king of Egypt. Deuteronomy 7:7-8*

💬 How do these two scriptures reveal God's emotions? What emotions does he feel? Can you think of any other examples?

Emotional Beings

Feelings can be useful as they inform us of actions or direction that we might need to take but if we walk our Christian lives based only on how we feel, we won't get very far.

📖 *Finally, be strong in the Lord and in his mighty power. Put on the full armour of God, so that you can take your stand against the devil's schemes. For our struggle is not against flesh and blood, but against the rulers, against the authorities, against the powers of this dark world and against the spiritual forces of evil in the heavenly realms. Therefore put on the full armour of God, so that when the day of evil comes, you may be able to stand your ground, and after you have done everything, to stand. Stand firm then, with the belt of truth buckled round your waist, with the breastplate of righteousness in place, and with your feet fitted with the readiness that comes from the gospel of peace. In addition to all this, take up the shield of faith, with which you can extinguish all the flaming arrows of the evil one. Take the helmet of salvation and the sword of the Spirit, which is the word of God. Ephesians 6:10-17*

📖 *He has sent me to bind up the broken-hearted,*
to proclaim freedom for the captives
and release from darkness for the prisoners. Isaiah 61

Emotional Beings

Knowing that we can walk into different situations and be taken captive by an atmosphere that isn't ours is important. The enemy loves it when we begin to own negative atmospheres that were never ours. Ephesians 6 tells us that we need to stand firm. This starts with discerning the environment that we are in and if atmospheres try to attach themselves to us we can deal with this by refusing it and telling it to 'get lost'.

Have you any experience of this or how could you guard your life against it?

Then Peter came to Jesus and asked, 'Lord, how many times shall I forgive my brother or sister who sins against me? Up to seven times?' Jesus answered, 'I tell you, not seven times, but seventy-seven times. 'Therefore, the kingdom of heaven is like a king who wanted to settle accounts with his servants. As he began the settlement, a man who owed him ten thousand bags of gold was brought to him. Since he was not able to pay, the master ordered that he and his wife and his children and all that he had be sold to repay the debt. 'At this the servant fell on his knees before him. "Be patient with me," he begged, "and I will pay back everything." The servant's master took pity on

Emotional Beings

him, cancelled the debt, and let him go. 'But when that servant went out, he found one of his fellow servants who owed him a hundred silver coins He grabbed him and began to choke him. "Pay back what you owe me!" he demanded. 'His fellow servant fell to his knees and begged him, "Be patient with me, and I will pay it back." 'But he refused. Instead, he went off and had the man thrown into prison until he could pay the debt. When the other servants saw what had happened, they were outraged and went and told their master everything that had happened. 'Then the master called the servant in. "You wicked servant," he said, "I cancelled all that debt of yours because you begged me to. Shouldn't you have had mercy on your fellow servant just as I had on you?" In anger his master handed him over to the jailers to be tortured, until he should pay back all he owed. 'This is how my heavenly Father will treat each of you unless you forgive your brother or sister from your heart.' Matthew 18:21-35

This is a parable that Jesus taught regarding how we become prisoners.

Jesus told us it is essential that we live in forgiveness. To not do so is akin to making ourselves prisoners. It's like being in a jail cell with the keys within reach and choosing not to take them.

💬 **Have you got any testimony of when you were able to forgive, and it set you free? What was this like? What was the difference before and afterwards?**

If you are believing things about yourself, or have owned things that aren't yours, there are some simple steps that you can take to work this through. When you renounce the lie if there are people you need to forgive you should do it then so that you can receive the truth!

PRAYING FOR INNER HEALING
- **W**hat lie am I believing
- **A**sk for the truth
- **R**enounce the lie and receive the truth
- **M**ove forward

Use this stepped process within the group and pray for one another. Remember if you still feel stuck there are ministries like Healing Rooms and Bethel Sozo you can access.

ABOUT THE AUTHOR

Alastair works for Tricordant, a Christian-based organisational consultancy, which he helped found in 2005. He enjoys working with a diverse range of clients as a consultant – from the NHS and councils to international NGOs and global companies. Prior to that he spent fifteen years in NHS senior management, including as a Chief Executive. He's also been a Non-Executive Director in the NHS for thirteen years, a Visiting Fellow at Brunel Business School, and co-founder and Treasurer of the European Organisation Design Forum. He has an MA in Natural Sciences (Biochemistry) from the University of Cambridge and post-graduate diplomas in Philosophy and Healthcare, and Health Services Management, and an NTL Organisation Development Certificate.

Alastair has been a Christian since he was a teenager. He spent a year after university working as a Careforce volunteer for an Anglican church in Corby before moving to Reading and joining the NHS. Alastair has lived in Reading, England, since 1987, where he met and married his wife Jane, a primary school/nursery teacher. They have been married for over twenty-eight years and have two grown-up sons, Adam and David.

For the last sixteen years he's been an Elder at The Gate (formerly Reading Community Church/Tilehurst Free Church) where he's involved in leadership, preaching, and healing ministry. He is a Global Awakening Certified Healing Practitioner and a member of Agape Freedom Fighters ministry. He is also Moderator of the Baptist Union of Great Britain.

For fun he enjoys painting, chess, canoeing, running (nothing more than a few Reading half-marathons), and watching sport – including Reading and Spurs football teams.

CONTACT DETAILS FOR THE ARTISTS

The following artists were kind enough to donate their artwork for use in this book. You can find out more about each artist using these links. The next page gices a refernce guide for each picture, with some extra notes.

Rebecca Jesty
facebook.com/jesty.art

Sam Horne
samhorneart.co.uk

Ralph Mann
purpleheron.co.uk

Yinka Oyekan
facebook.com/PrinceAdeyinkaOyekan

Rebecca Machin and Jenny Whitfield
via thegate.uk.com

PRAYER

We hope you enjoyed this book and that is has been both a blessing and a challenge to your life and walk with God. Maybe you just got hold of it and are looking through before starting. Long ago, we made the decision never to take for granted that everyone has prayed a prayer to receive Jesus as their Lord, so we're including that as the finale to this book. If you have never asked Jesus into your life and would like to do that now, it's so easy. Just pray this simple prayer:

Dear Lord Jesus, thank You for dying on the cross for me. I believe that You gave Your life so that I could have life. When You died on the cross, You died as an innocent man who had done nothing wrong. You were paying for my sins and the debt I could never pay. I believe in You, Jesus, and receive the brand new life and fresh start that the Bible promises that I can have. Thank You for my sins forgiven, for the righteousness that comes to me as a gift from You, for hope and love beyond what I have known and the assurance of eternal life that is now mine. Amen.

Good next moves are to get yourself a Bible that is easy to understand and begin to read. Maybe start in John so you can discover all about Jesus for yourself. Start to pray – prayer is simply talking to God – and, finally, find a church that's alive and get your life planted in it. These simple ingredients will cause your relationship with God to grow.

Why not email us and let us know if you did that so we can rejoice with you? Tell us about your redemption story.

The Great Big Life Publishing team,
info@greatbiglifepublishing.com

FURTHER INFORMATION

For further information about the author of this book, or to order more copies, please contact:

Great Big Life Publishing
Empower Centre
83-87 Kingston Road
Portsmouth
Hants
PO2 7DX
UK

info@greatbiglifepublishing.com
greatbiglifepublishing.com
@GBLPublishing

ARE YOU AN AUTHOR?

Do you have a Word from God on your heart that you're looking to get published to a wider audience? We're looking for manuscripts that identify with our own vision of bringing life-giving and relevant messages to the Body of Christ. Send yours for review towards possible publication to:

Great Big Life Publishing
Empower Centre
83-87 Kingston Road
Portsmouth
Hants
PO2 7DX
UK

or, email us at info@greatbiglifepublishing.com

Printed in Poland
by Amazon Fulfillment
Poland Sp. z o.o., Wrocław